Fire Fighter ENGLISH

소방공무원을 위한 현장생활영어

노이균 저

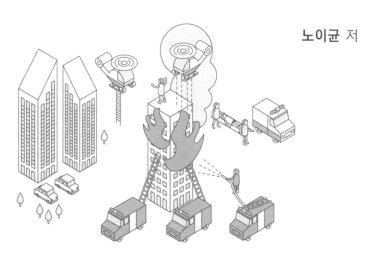

(주)백산출판사

머리말

이 책을 쓸 수 있도록 오늘의 나를 만들어 주신 하나님과 우리 부모님께 먼저 감사의 말씀을 드린다.

21년 동안 다양한 전공의 학생들을 강단에서 지도해 오면서 준비해 두었던 자료를 모아 오늘의 결실을 맺는다. 특히 학생들과 사회인들에게 생활영어를 지도해 오면서 축적해 두었던 33년의 know-how가 이 책을 만드는데 큰 힘이 되었다.

2012년부터 소방공무원영어시험이 종전의 방식에서 탈피해서 오롯이 소방생활영어중심으로 문제가 꾸준히 출제되어 왔다. 경찰·소방공무원시험 준비생의 96% 이상이 영어로 고생한다고 한다. 이 책을 통해 이러한 수치가 줄어들 수 있도록 기도하는 마음으로 이 책을 완성했다.

이 책은 Teaching of Response Guidebook, Teaching of English for Firefighters, Fundamentals of Fire Fighter Skills, 그리고 Essentials of Fire Fighting 등의 책에서 많은 도움을 받았다. 그리고 의학적 도움은 강동경희대학병원 응급학과 김명천 교수님으로부터 받았다. 김명천 교수님께 감사의 마음을 드린다. 아울러 오늘의 결실을 맺게끔 도움을 주신 우송정보대학교 소방안전관리과 학과장이신 허만성 교수님께도 감사의 말씀을 드린다.

　꼼꼼한 교정을 해준 딸 사라와 드러나지 않게 내조하고 기도로 도와주며 동역해 오고 있는 집사람과 늘 아빠를 지지·격려해주는 든든한 아들 요한이에게 고마운 마음을 전한다.

2018년 7월 17일

관악산을 바라보며

松巖 노이균 씀

차례

CONTENTS

소방 관련 필수 · 핵심 용어

I

PART 01 소방 기구
(Fire Fighting Departments)

소방서
- Fire station

119 구조대
- 119 rescue service

119 안전센터
- 119 safety center

중앙 119 구조본부
- National 119 rescue headquarters

중앙소방학교
- National fire service academy

수난구조대
- Water rescue company[1]

산악구조대

- ○ Mountain rescue company

특별구조대

- ○ Special rescue company

삼림 소방대원

- ○ Smoke jumper

소방행정과

- ○ Fire administration section

방호과 · 화재진압과

- ○ Fire suppression section

화재구조과

- ○ Fire rescue section

화재예방과

- ○ Fire prevention section

의용소방대

- ○ Volunteer fire substation

---

1) 구조대는 rescue team[party, unit, squad] 등으로 불린다.

15 국립방재교육연구원

- ● National disaster management institute

16 국립방재연구원

- ● National institute for disaster prevention

m / e / m / o

PART 02 계급
(Ranks)

소방총감
- Fire commissioner

소방정감
- Fire marshal

소방감
- Deputy chief

소방준감
- Deputy assistant chief/Deputy fire marshal

소방령
- Second lieutenant/Assistant fire chief

소방경
- Battalion chief/Fire captain

7. 소방위

○ Senior captain/Fire lieutenant

8. 소방장

○ Captain/Fire sergeant

9. 소방교

○ Senior fire fighter

10. 소방사

○ Fire fighter/Fireman

11. 소방사 시보

○ Fire recruit

m / e / m / o

PART 03 구조장비
(Rescue Equipment)

1 소방차
- Fire engine/Fire truck

2 견인차
- Wrecker/Tow truck[2]

3 고가 사다리
- Aerial ladder

4 공기식 구조매트
- Air cushion rescue mattress

5 공기톱
- Air saw/Pneumatic saw

---

2) 영국에서는 breakdown truck[lorry]라고 부른다.

6 체인톱

- Chain saw

7 소화기

- Fire extinguisher

8 공기호흡기

- Air breathing apparatus/Air respiratory machine

9 산소호흡기

- Oxygen breathing apparatus/Oxygen respiratory breather

10 구조복

- Rescue suit

11 권양기

- Winch[3]

12 들것

- Stretcher

13 등강기

- Ascender[4]

---

3) 원통형의 드럼에 와이어 로프를 감았다 풀었다 함으로써 물건을 위아래로 옮기는 기계.
4) 고정된 로프를 타고 오르기 위해 사용되는 기계적 장치. 주마(jumar) 또는 어센더라고도 부른

하강기

- Descender

로프

- Rope

방화복

- Fire suit/Fire-proof uniform

보호안경

- Goggles

안전벨트

- Safety belt

에어백

- Air bag

소방용 가스 마스크 · 방독면

- smoke helmet

다. 주로 대암벽에서 인공등반 또는 짐을 끌어올리거나 신속한 등반을 위해 쓰인다. 이 외에도 확보를 하거나 추락자 고정, 부상자 구조에도 쓰이며 히말라야와 같은 고산의 위험 구간에 설치한 고정로프를 이용하여 등반할 때도 사용된다. 1959년 스위스의 가이드 유시(Jusi)와 공학박사 말티(Marti)가 개발했으며, 최초의 고안자 두 사람의 이름을 붙여 '주마'라는 상품명으로 했다. '주마'는 스위스 등강기 제조사의 브랜드일 뿐인데, 이 상품명이 오늘날 등강기의 대명사처럼 되어버렸다.

21 열화상카메라

- Thermographic camera/Thermal imaging camera[5]

22 유압도어오프너

- Hydraulic door opener[6]

23 유압전개기

- Hydraulic arm spreader[7]

24 유압절단기

- Hydraulic cutter

25 유압펌프

- Hydraulic pump

---

5) 열화상카메라는 열을 추적, 탐지하여 화면으로 한눈에 보여주는 장치를 말한다. 일반 카메라는 사람의 눈과 같은 구조를 하고 있어 우리 눈이 보는 것과 유사한 모습을 담아내지만 열화상카메라는 오직 열을 이용해서 촬영하는 특수 장비이다. 멀리서는 눈에 보이지 않을 정도의 작은 화재라고 해도, 열화상카메라는 이것을 포착할 수 있다. 또한 가축의 질병 여부를 손쉽게 판단하는데도 사용된다. 다른 가축에 비해 특별히 열이 더 있는 것으로 관찰되는 가축은 병에 걸렸을 가능성이 높기 때문이다. 군사용으로도 사용되는데, 열화상카메라를 이용하면 빛이 전혀 없는 밤이라고 할지라도 스스로 열을 발생시키는 사람의 몸을 쉽게 찾아낼 수 있어 야간 감시 장비로 사용된다. 이처럼 열화상카메라는 열을 어느 정도 내는지에 따라서 화면을 보여 주기 때문에 연기와 같은 장애물의 유무, 빛의 유무와 상관없이 물체를 확인할 수 있다.

6) 화재 및 구조 긴급 상황 발생 시 자물쇠나 방화문 등을 강제로 개방하여 구조대원이 진입하는 데 사용하는 장비임.

7) 집게방식으로 사고 난 차량의 문짝을 벌리는 기계.

이동식발전기
- Portable generator

인명구조경보기
- Rescue alarm

지렛대
- Lever

차단기
- Breaker

착암기
- Rock drill[8]

케이블절단기
- Cable cutter/Wire cutter

---

8) 암석을 폭파하기 위한 폭약을 장전(裝塡)하는 구멍(발파구멍)을 만드는 기계.

PART 04 구급장비
(First-aid Equipment)

1. 검안라이트
- Eye examination light/Pen light

2. 골절부목
- Fracture splint

3. 공기부목
- Air splint

4. 구강기도유지기
- Oral airway supporter

5. 비강기도유지기
- Nasal airway supporter

6. 방독면조정끈 · 머리고정대
- Head harness

목고정대

○ Neck harness

분리형 들것

○ Separable stretcher/Detachable stretcher

붕대

○ Bandage[9]

시체 운반용 포대

○ Body bag

생리식염수

○ Saline solution

인공호흡기

○ Resuscitator/Respirator

제세동기

○ Cardioverter/Defibrillator[10]

---

9) 붕대의 종류에는 일반용(regular), 압박용(compress), 화상용(burn) 등이 있다.

10) 부정맥을 보이는 심장에 고압전류를 극히 단시간 통하게 함으로써 정상적인 맥박으로 회복시키는 기기를 제세동기라고 한다.

14 심전도 모니터

- Electrocardiogram monitor

15 아트로핀 · 경련 완화제

- Atropine

16 지혈대

- Tourniquet

17 척추고정판

- Spine supporter/Spine board

18 온도계

- Thermometer

19 혈압계

- Blood pressure gauge/Tonometer/Sphygmomanometer

20 후두경

- Laryngoscope[11]

---

11) 입속에 깊숙이 넣어 후두 부위를 관찰하는 데 쓰이는 거울. 가늘고 긴 자루에 작은 거울이 달렸다.

PART 05 응급치료 용어
(First-aid Terms)

가스중독
- Gas poisoning

경련
- Convulsion/Spasm

골절
- Fracture

두개골 골절
- Skull fracture

두부손상
- Head injury

골반골절
- Pelvis fracture

7 개방성골절

- Open fracture

8 폐쇄성골절

- Close fracture

9 두개골 골절

- Skull fracture

10 다발성 늑골 골절

- Complex rib fracture

11 부정맥

- Irregular pulse · heartbeat/Unequal pulse·heartbeat

12 공황

- Panic

13 과민방응

- Allergic reaction

14 과민성 쇼크

- Hypersensitive shock/Anaphylactic shock[12]

---

12) 특정한 항원에 접촉한 뒤 수 분에서 수 시간 내에 발생하는 쇼크.

15 대사성 쇼크
- Metabolic shock

16 관통상
- Penetrating wound

17 근육
- Muscle

18 기관절개
- Tracheotomy

19 기도폐쇄
- Respiratory obstruction/Airway blockage

20 동상
- Frostbite

21 두통
- Headache

22 복부
- Abdomen

23 부상자

- Wounded · Injured person/The injured·wounded

24 사망자

- The dead

25 산소공급

- Oxygenation/Oxygen supply

26 삽관법

- Intubation[13]

27 삽입

- Insertion

28 생식기 장애

- Genital trouble

29 표피외상

- Epidermal external wound/Skin·Surface trauma

30 혈뇨

- Hematuria/Red water

---

13) 환부에 꽂아 액을 빼내거나 약을 넣는 데 쓰는 금속관은 cannula라고 한다.

협심증

   ⊙ Angina

혈압

   ⊙ Blood pressure

고혈압

   ⊙ High blood pressure/Hypertension

저혈압

   ⊙ Low blood pressure/Hypotension

혈액순환

   ⊙ Blood circulation

인공호흡

   ⊙ Artificial respiration/CPR/Mouth-to-mouth resuscitation[14]

혼수 · 혼미 · 인사불성

   ⊙ Stupor/coma/lethargy/unconscious state

1도 · 2도 · 3도 화상

   ⊙ First-degree · Second-degree·Third-degree burn

---

14) CPR = Cardiopulmonary Resuscitation(심폐소생술)

39 **활력징후**

　◐ Vital sign

40 **흉부압박**

　◐ Chest compression

41 **흡입**

　◐ Suction

42 **격분 · 흥분**

　◐ Agitation

m / e / m / o

PART 06 재난 관련 용어
(Terms Relevant to Disaster)

황사
- Yellow dust · sand/Asian dust

가뭄
- Drought

장마
- Rainy season

홍수
- Flood/Deluge

폭설
- Heavy snow

폭우 · 호우
- Heavy rain/Torrential rain/Downpour

7 호우경보

○ Heavy rain warning/Heavy rain watch/Heavy rain alert

8 집중호우

○ Localized heavy rain/Localized torrential downpours

9 폭염

○ Heat wave/Scorching heat

10 폭염주의보

○ Heat wave warning/Heat wave watch/Heat wave alert

11 강풍

○ Strong wind/Gale

12 돌풍

○ Gust/Squall

13 한파

○ Cold wave

14 강우량

○ Rainfall/Precipitation

15 강설량

- Snowfall

16 낙뢰

- Lightning/Thunderbolt

17 눈사태

- Avalanche

18 산사태

- Landslide

19 지진

- Earthquake

20 진앙 · 진원

- Epicenter

21 해일

- Tsunami/Tidal wave

22 화산재

- Volcanic ash

23 대기오염

- Air pollution/Air contamination

24 태풍

- Typhoon

m / e / m / o

PART 07 소방 관련 용어
(Terms Relevant to Fire Fighting)

건물도면 · 청사진
○ Building drawing/Blueprint

건물구조
○ Building structure

고층건물
○ Skyscraper/High-rise

구조대
○ Rescue team

구조방법
○ Rescue method

구조작업
○ Rescue operation

7 대피

○ Evacuation

8 매몰 · 매장

○ Burial

9 환기구

○ Vent

10 반소(半燒)하다

○ Be half burned/Be partially burned down

11 전소(全燒)하다

○ Be completely burned down

12 발화점

○ Ignition point[15]

13 자연발화

○ Spontaneous ignition

---

15) 1. 공기 중에서 물질을 가열할 때 스스로 발화하여 연소를 시작하는 최저 온도.
    2. 화재 원인을 알아볼 때, 화재를 일으킨 자리를 이르는 말.

인화점
- Flashing point[16)

연소점
- Fire point[17)

직사주수
- Straight stream

진화작업
- Putting out the fire

초기진화
- Initial extinguishment

지하층
- Basement floor

폭발
- Explosion

---

16) 어떤 물질이 불붙을 수 있는 최저 온도.
17) 제품이 표준화된 시험 조건에서 발화하고 그 표면에 작은 화염으로 열이 가해진 후에 명시된 시간 동안 계속해서 탈 수 있는 가장 낮은 온도.

21 방화
  - Arson

22 감전
  - Electric shock

23 불꽃
  - Flame

24 비상구
  - Fire exit/Emergency exit

25 비상조명
  - Emergency light

26 소방검사
  - Fire inspection

27 화재 대피 훈련
  - Fire drill

28 화인(火因) · 화재원인
  - Cause of fire

29 화재감시인

- ⚙ Fire guard

30 인명구조

- ⚙ Life rescue

31 사상자 · 인명피해

- ⚙ Casualties

m / e / m / o

Ⅰ 소방 관련 기초 용어 문제

01 소방서

Fire Station[Department]

02 위급 · 비상사태

emergency

03 위치

location

04 휘발성 물질

volatile material

05 1도 화상

first-degree burn

06 견인차

Answer wrecker/tow truck

07 고가 사다리

Answer aerial ladder

08 비상구

emergency   /fire

Answer exit/escape

09 119구조대

119   Service

Answer Rescue

10 발화점

point

Answer ignition

11 인화점

point

Answer flashing

12 의용소방대

fire substation

Answer volunteer

13 인명피해

Answer casualties

14 소방차

Answer fire engine[truck]

15 소방사

fire

Answer fighter

16 방화

Answer arson

17 소화기

Answer fire extinguisher

18 초기진화

early stage _____ /initial

Answer suppression/extinguishment

19 화재원인 · 화인(火因)

_____ of fire

Answer cause

20 대피하라

take _____ /evacuate

Answer shelter

21 방화복

Answer fire-proof uniform/fire suit

22 권양기

Answer winch

23 인공호흡

Answer artificial respiration/CPR/mouth-to-mouth resuscitation

24 국립방재연구원

Answer national institute for disaster prevention

m / e / m / o

사고 유형별
필수 문장

Ⅱ

PART 01 소방
(Fire Fighting)

○ 소방공무원을 위한 현장영어회화집 ○

1. 화재신고 시 소방대원이 암기해야 할 필수 문장
(The Compulsory Sentences for Fire Fighters with a Fire Report)

1 119입니다. 상황을 말씀해 보세요.18)

- This is 119. What's your emergency?
- 119. State your emergency.
- 119. How may I help you?
- 119. What's the matter?

2 불이 어디서 났습니까?

- Where is the fire?
- Where is the fire located?
- Where did the fire start?

---

18) 소방서에서 신고 전화를 받고 소방차를 파견하는 사람을 dispatcher라고 한다. 이 사람이 신고전화를 받고 응대할 때 가장 전형적인 표현이 바로 "What's your emergency?" 또는 "State your emergency."이다. 직역하면 "당신의 긴급 상황이 무엇입니까?" "당신의 긴급 상황을 말씀해 보세요."라는 뜻이 되지만, 일반적으로 이와 같은 119 상황에서는 "무엇을 도와 드릴까요?"라는 의미로 해석한다.

불이 어떻게 난 건지 아십니까?

◕ Do you know how the fire started?

화재 규모는 어떻습니까?

◕ How large is the fire?

주택[아파트, 공장, 사무실, 차량]에서 불이 난 겁니까?

◕ Is the house[apartment, factory, office, car] on fire?

무엇을 만드는 공장입니까?

◕ What kind of factory is it?

건물내부에 위험물이 있습니까?

◕ Are there any dangerous materials inside the building?

폭발물질이 있습니까?

◕ Are there any explosives?

◕ Are there any explosive materials?

몇 층짜리 건물입니까?

◕ How tall is the building?

◕ How many stories high is the building?

몇 층에서 화재가 났습니까?

◕ Which floor is on fire?

What floor is the fire on?

11 불꽃이 보입니까?

Can you see the flame?

12 사람들은 다 대피했나요?

Has everyone been evacuated?

13 건물에 남아 있는 사람이 있나요?

Are there any people still left in the building?

14 인명구조가 필요합니까?

Do people need to be rescued?

15 출입구는 어디죠?

Where is the exit?

16 출입구가 여기 말고 또 있나요?

Is there another exit other than this one?

17 소방차가 출동 중입니다.

Fire trucks are on their way.

18 소방차가 방금 출동했습니다.

The fire engine has just left.

즉시 출동하겠습니다.

- We will send fire fighters right away.

도착하려면 5분 정도 걸립니다.

- It will take about 5 minutes to get there.

실례지만 성함과 전화번호는 어떻게 되십니까?

- Can I have your name and phone number, please?

연락 가능한 번호가 몇 번입니까?

- What number can I reach you?

전화를 끊지 마세요.

- Don't hang up, please.
- Hang on the line.
- Hold the line.

전화를 받아 주시고 안내해 주세요.19)

- Don't miss the call and show them the way, please.

소방차가 보이면 안내를 해 주세요.

- When you see the fire engine, show them the way, please.

19) 장난전화는 prank call이라고 한다.

26 사이렌 소리가 들리면, 안내해 주세요.

⊙ When you hear the siren, show them the way, please.

2. 화재현장에서 소방대원이 암기해야 할 필수 문장
(The Compulsory Sentences for Fire Fighters at the Scene of a Fire)

1 몇 가지 질문 좀 하겠습니다.

⊙ May I ask you some questions?

2 화재신고 하신 분이 누구십니까?

⊙ Who is the one that reported the fire?

3 당신이 화재 최초 목격자이십니까?

⊙ Are you the first witness of the fire?

4 천천히 말씀해 주세요.

⊙ Speak slowly, please.

5 진정하시고 다시 한 번 말씀해 주세요.

⊙ Calm down and repeat that, please.

6 자, 좀 물러나시고 진정하세요.

⊙ Back off a little and stay[remain] calm[cool], please.

화재 발생 시 비상벨이 울렸나요?

○ Did the fire alarm go off when the fire started?

협조해 주셔서 고맙습니다.

○ Thank you for your cooperation.

3. 아파트 화재신고 시 소방대원이 암기해야 할 필수 문장
(The Compulsory Sentences for Fire Fighters with an Apartment Fire Report)

119입니다. 무엇을 도와 드릴까요?

○ 119. What is your emergency?

어디서 불이 났나요, 선생님?

○ Where is the fire, sir?

연기가 많이 발생하나요?

○ Do you see a lot of smoke?

불꽃이랑 연기가 많이 납니까?

○ Can you see any flames and smoke?

근처에 사람이 있나요?

○ Do you see anyone around you?

6 우선 선생님이 진정하는 것이 중요합니다.

◑ First of all, it is important (that) you (should) stay calm.

7 불이 난 곳은 아파트 몇 동 몇 호인가요?

◑ What is the apartment number where the fire is located?

8 지금 소방차를 가급적 빨리 출동시키겠습니다.

◑ A fire engine will be there as soon as possible.

9 전화를 끊지 마세요.

◑ Hold the line, please.

10 우리가 도착하기 전에 계단을 이용해서 사람들을 대피시켜 주세요.

◑ Please take the stairs and evacuate people from the building before we get there.

11 신고해 주셔서 고맙습니다.

◑ Thank you for your call.

12 소방차가 출동 중에 있습니다.

◑ Fire engines are on their way.

PART 02 구조
(Rescue)

1. 교통사고 신고 시 구조대원이 암기해야 할 필수 문장
(The Compulsory Sentences for Rescue Workers with a Traffic Accident Report)

방배소방서 구조대입니다. 무엇을 도와드릴까요?

- This is a rescue team from Bangbae Fire Station. How can I help you?

사고가 난 장소가 어디입니까?

- Where did the accident occur?
- Where is the location of the accident?

어떤 종류의 사고입니까?

- What kind of accident is it?

다중 충돌입니까?

- Is it a multiple collision?

5 정면충돌입니까?

○ Is it a head-on collision?

6 후미추돌 사고입니까?

○ Is it a rear-end crash?

7 어떻게 사고가 났습니까, 선생님?

○ How did the accident happen, sir?

8 다치신 분이 있습니까?

○ Are there any people injured?

○ Is anybody hurt?

9 몇 명이 다치셨습니까?

○ How many people have been injured?

10 차안에 갇혀 있는 분이 계신가요?

○ Is there anyone stuck in the car?

11 그분은 의식이 있습니까?

○ Is he/she conscious?

12 그분은 출혈이 심합니까?

○ Is he/she bleeding badly?

13 그분은 움직일 수 있습니까?

◎ Can he/she move?

14 주변에 교통 표지판이 보입니까?

◎ Are there any traffic signs nearby?

◎ Can you see any traffic signs around you?

15 주변에 큰 건물이 있습니까?

◎ Are there any big buildings around you?

◎ Is there any landmark near you?

16 구조대가 도착할 때까지 환자의 몸을 따뜻하게 해 주십시오.

◎ Please keep the victim's body warm until rescuers arrive.

17 구조대와 구급차를 바로 보내 드리겠습니다.

◎ We will send you a rescue team and an ambulance right away.

18 잠시만 기다리시면 곧 구조해 드리겠습니다.

◎ We will rescue you in a minute.

19 구조차량이 출동 중입니다.

◎ The rescue car is on the way.

20 구급대가 가고 있습니다.

◎ The paramedics are on the way.

2. 교통사고 현장에서 구조대원이 암기해야 할 필수 문장
(The Compulsory Sentences for Rescue Workers at the Scene of a Traffic Accident)

관악소방서 구급대원입니다.

◎ This is a paramedic from Gwanak Fire Station.

사고가 어떻게 발생했는지 기억이 납니까?

◎ Do you remember how the accident happened[occurred]?

◎ Do you remember anything about the car accident?

사고 후 시간이 얼마나 지났습니까?

◎ How long has it been since the accident?

움직이지 마시고 가만히 계십시오.

◎ Do not move and stay[remain] still.

움직이면 상태가 악화될 수 있습니다.

◎ Moving might worsen the injury.

아프시면 말씀하세요.

◎ Please tell me if it hurts.

어디를 다치셨습니까?

◎ Where were you injured?

어디가 아프세요?

⊙ Where does it hurt?

어떻게 다치셨습니까?

⊙ How were you injured?

어떻게 아프세요?

⊙ How does it hurt?

통증이 심합니까?

⊙ Does it hurt a lot?

어느 부분이 가장 아프십니까?

⊙ Where do you feel the most pain?

⊙ Where does it hurt most?

선생님은 괜찮으세요?

⊙ Are you O.K., sir?

발목에 부목을 대고 들것으로 옮기겠습니다.

⊙ I am going to apply a splint to your ankle and then carry you on a stretcher.

구급차량으로 옮기겠습니다.

⊙ I will move you to an ambulance.

16 이제 구조작업을 시작하겠습니다.

- ⊙ We will now launch rescue operations.
- ⊙ We are going to engage in rescue operations.

17 이제 곧 병원에 도착합니다.

- ⊙ We will soon arrive at the hospital.

m / e / m / o

PART 03 소방검사 및 화재조사
(Fire Inspection & Investigation)

1. 소방검사(Fire Inspection)

안녕하십니까? 저는 대전소방서 예방과에서 나온 소방관 ○○○입니다.

　○ Hello. My name is ○○○. I am a fire fighter from the Fire Prevention Section, Daejeon Fire Station.

소방검사를 하러 이곳에 나왔습니다.

　○ I am here to conduct[do] a fire inspection.

건물 층수 및 면적이 어떻게 됩니까?

　○ How many stories are there in this building and what is the floor space?

근무 인원은 몇 명입니까?

　○ How many people work here?

5 소방시설은 정상적으로 작동되고 있습니까?

- Does the fire extinguishing equipment work well[properly]?
- Are the fire extinguishing facilities working well?

6 건물 내에 설치된 피난기구는 무엇이 있습니까?

- What kind of fire escape equipment is installed in the building?

7 자동화재 경보설비와 자동화재 탐지기는 어디에 있습니까?

- Where are the automatic alarm system and automatic fire detector?

8 옥내 소화전 및 스프링클러 설비 펌프실은 어디에 있습니까?

- Where are the indoor fire extinguishers and the sprinkler pump room?

9 위험물 및 화기 취급 시 안전수칙을 잘 지켜 주십시오.

- Please follow the fire safety regulations for explosives and flammable materials strictly.

10 소방검사는 2년에 한 번 실시합니다.

- The fire inspection is conducted once in every 2 years.

경미한 지적사항에 대해서는 빠른 시일 내에 정비하시기 바랍니다.

◎ Please correct the minor problems we have listed for you as soon as possible.

소방검사에 임하여 주셔서 감사합니다.

◎ Thank you for your cooperation with the fire inspection.

2. 화재조사
(Fire Investigation)

안녕하십니까? 저는 서초소방서 화재조사관 ○○○입니다.

◎ Hello. I am a fire investigator, ○○○, with Seocho Fire Department.

화재를 신고하셨습니까?

◎ Did you report the fire?

화재를 목격하셨습니까?

◎ Did you witness the fire?

화재가 어디서부터 시작되었습니까?

◎ Where did the fire start?

5 화재 당시 어디서 무엇을 하고 계셨습니까?

○ Where were you and what were you doing when noticed the fire?

6 화재 발생 사실을 어떻게 아셨습니까?

○ How did you find[know] there was a fire?

7 화재 당시 상황이 어땠습니까?

○ What was it like when you noticed the fire?

8 화재경보기가 울리면 즉시 건물에서 나가십시오.

○ If the fire alarm goes off, please leave the building quickly.

9 폭발음이나 이상한 소리가 들렸습니까?

○ Did you hear any explosions or other strange sounds?

10 화재 당시 화약류 또는 위험물질을 취급하셨습니까?

○ Were you using any explosives or other dangerous materials when the fire started?

11 화재 당시 경보설비가 제대로 작동되었습니까?

○ Did the fire alarm work properly at the time of the fire?

12 화재로 부상을 당한 사람이 있습니까?

- ○ Was anyone injured by the fire?

13 어디를 얼마나 다쳤습니까?

- ○ How much and where were you hurt?

14 환자는 어느 병원으로 이송했습니까?

- ○ Which hospital was the patient sent[transferred] to?

15 이 건물은 누구의 소유입니까?

- ○ Who owns this building?
- ○ Who does this building belong to?

16 소유자의 연락처를 알려 주십시오.

- ○ Please let me know the phone number of the owner.
- ○ Please tell me the phone number of the owner.

17 화재보험을 가입했나요?[20)

- ○ Do you have a fire insurance?

18 어느 보험사입니까?

- ○ What's the name of the insurance company?

---

20) 생명보험(life insurance), 재해보험(casualty insurance), 자동차보험(automobile insurance)

19 당신의 이름과 주민등록번호를 알려 주십시오.

- Please tell me your name and resident registration number
- Please let me know your name and I.D. number.

20 화재와 관련하여 도움이 필요하시면 말씀하십시오.

- Let me know if you need any help related to the fire.

21 협조해 주셔서 고맙습니다.

- Thank you for your cooperation.

m / e / m / o

PART 04 **재난 관련 기타 문장**
(Other Sentences Relevant to Disaster)

서울시 재난안전 대책본부에서 알려드립니다.

- This is an announcement from the Disaster Safety Center of Seoul City.

TV 또는 라디오의 기상상황을 주의 깊게 청취하십시오.

- Listen carefully to the TV or radio for the weather conditions.

한반도 지역은 태풍의 영향 하에 놓여 있습니다.

- The Korean peninsula is under a typhoon threat.

오늘 경주 지역 일대에 진도 4.5의 지진이 발생하였다.[21]

- A 4.5 (magnitude) earthquake struck[hit] some areas in Gyeongju today.

---

21) 4.5 = four point five라고 읽는다.

5 이 지역은 건물 붕괴로 인해 여전히 위험한 상태입니다.

○ This area is still in danger due to a collapsed building.

6 해일이 오후 6시경 제주 해안에 도착할 것입니다.

○ The tsunami[tidal wave] will hit the coast of Jeju around 6 p.m.

7 그곳은 위험지역이므로 대피하여야 합니다.

○ You are in a dangerous area. You need to evacuate.

8 가벼운 생필품과 돈, 중요한 서류 등을 챙기십시오.

○ Take some necessities, money and important documents.

9 해운대중학교에 대피소가 있습니다.

○ There is a shelter at Haeundae Middle School.

10 지진 발생 시 가스 밸브를 잠가 주시고 전기차단기를 내려주세요.

○ During earthquakes turn off all the gas valves and electricity breakers.

11 물이 계속 차오르면 높은 곳으로 대피하십시오.

○ Evacuate to a higher place if the water level keeps rising.

12 건물의 출입문이나 창문은 모두 닫아 주십시오.

○ Close all the doors and windows in the building.

하수도 또는 맨홀이 있는 곳에는 가까이 가지 마십시오.

  ⊙ Do not go near manholes or sewers.

전신주, 가로등을 손으로 만지지 마십시오.22)

  ⊙ Do not touch electric poles and street lamps[lights].

번개가 칠 경우 건물 밖으로 나오지 마십시오.

  ⊙ In case of lightning, remain inside the building.

승강기는 이용하지 마십시오.

  ⊙ Do not use elevators[lifts].

가방이나 방석으로 머리를 보호하십시오.

  ⊙ Protect and cover your head with a bag or cushion.

책상 밑이나 욕실로 잠시 피하십시오.

  ⊙ Seek[take, find] shelter under a desk or inside a bathroom tub.

만약 유해가스가 있다면 젖은 수건이나 옷으로 코와 입을 막고 바닥을 기어 문 쪽으로 가십시오.

  ⊙ If there is harmful gas, cover your nose and mouth with a wet towel or your clothes and crawl along the floor to the door.

---

22) 가로등은 lamp post라고도 한다.

사고 유형별 필수 영어 문장 문제

PART 01 소방(Fire Fighting)

01 불이 어디서 났습니까?

Where is the fire _____?

Where did the fire _____?

_____ is the fire?

Answer located/start/Where

02 몇 층에서 불이 난거죠?

What _____ is the fire on?

Which floor is _____ fire?

Answer floor/on

03 화재 규모가 어떻습니까?

How _____ is the fire?

Answer large

04 불꽃이랑 연기가 많이 납니까?

Do you see a lot of _____ and _____?

Answer flames/smoke

05 아파트 몇 동 몇 층에서 불이 난 겁니까?

What's the apartment number _____ the fire is located?

Answer where

06 산중턱 같아요.

I guess it's the _____ of the mountain.

Answer middle

07 불이 어떻게 났는지 아십니까?

Do you know _____ the fire started?

Answer how

08 대피로[비상구]가 이 곳 말고 다른 곳이 있나요?

Is there any other _____?

Answer fire escape/emergency exit

09 사람들은 대피했나요?

Are all the people _____?

Answer evacuated

10 지금 계신 위치가 어디입니까?

Where is your current _____?

What's your _____?

Answer   location

11   주위에 교통 표지판이 있습니까?

Are there any _____ around there?

Answer   traffic signs

12   주위에 눈에 들어오는 큰 건물이 있나요?

Is there any _____ around you?

Answer   landmark

13   연락 가능한 전화번호가 어떻게 되세요?

What number can I _____ you?

Can I _____ your phone number?

Answer   reach/have

14   소방대원들이 출동하면서 전화를 할 테니 전화 받아 주세요.

Firefighters will _____ you when they are on their way.

Please do not _____ the call.

Answer   call/miss

15   소방차가 방금 출동했습니다.

The fire engine has just _____ .

Answer   left

16 도착하려면 5분 정도 걸립니다.

It will _____ about 5 minutes to _____ there.

Answer take/get

17 전화를 잘못 거셨습니다. 여기는 소방서입니다.

You have the _____ number.

This is a fire _____.

Answer wrong/department[station]

18 몇 층짜리 건물입니까?

How _____ is the building?

How many _____ high is the building?

Answer tall/stories

19 건물에 남아 있는 사람이 있습니까?

Are there any people still _____ in the building?

Answer left

20 사람들은 모두 대피했습니까?

Has everyone been _____ ?

Answer evacuated

21 화재가 확대될 가능성이 있습니까?

Is there any possibility the fire will _____ ?

Answer   spread

22 관계자분께 연락해 주십시오.

Please call the person who is in _____ .

Answer   charge

23 전화 끊지 마세요.

Please _____ the line.

Please _____ on the line

Pleases don't _____ .

Answer   hold/hang/hang up

24 당신을 그에게 바꿔 드릴게요.

I will put you _____ to him.

Answer   through

25 화재신고 하신 분이 누구세요?

Who is the one that _____ the fire?

Answer   reported

26 화재발생 시 비상벨이 울렸나요?

Did the fire alarm _____ when the fire started?

answer go off

27 화재 최초 목격자이십니까?

Are you the first _____ of the fire?

answer witness

m / e / m / o

PART 02 구조(Rescue)

01 통증이 심합니까?

Does it _____ badly?

Answer   hurt

02 아프시면 말씀하세요.

Tell me if it _____.

Answer   hurts

03 어느 부분이 가장 아프세요?

Where does it _____ most?

Where do you _____ the most pain?

Answer   hurt/feel

04 아픈 곳을 가리켜 보세요.

_____ to where it hurts.

Answer   Point

05 움직이지 말고 가만히 계세요.

Do not _____. please.

_____ still. please.

Answer   move/Stay

06 차 안에 갇혀 있는 분이 계세요?

Is there anyone _____ in the car?

Answer stuck

07 사고가 어떻게 일어났습니까?

How did the accident _____?

Answer occur[happen, take place]

08 정면충돌이었습니다.

It was a _____ collision.

Answer head-on

09 구조팀과 구급차를 즉시 보내겠습니다.

We will _____ a rescue team with an ambulance.

Answer dispatch

10 그 자동차는 빗길에 미끄러졌다.

The car _____ on the slippery road.

Answer skidded

11 사고 후 시간이 얼마나 지났습니까?

How long has it been _____ the accident?

Answer since

12 그녀는 발목을 삐었다.

She _____ her ankle.

Answer sprained

13 발목에 부목을 대겠습니다.

I am going to apply a _____ to your ankle.

Answer splint

14 선생님을 들것으로 옮기겠습니다.

I will carry you on a _____ .

Answer stretcher

15 내가 엘리베이터 안에 갇혔다.

I was _____ in an elevator.

Answer stuck

16 그는 의식은 있지만 출혈이 심하다.

He is _____ but he is _____ a lot.

Answer conscious/bleeding

17 지혈을 계속하세요.

Continue to _____ the bleeding.

Answer stop

18 그분은 몇 미터 높이에서 추락하셨나요?

How many meters _____ did he fall _____?

Answer high/from

19 우선 기계의 전원부터 차단시켜 주십시오.

First of all, _____ the power of the machine.

Answer turn off

20 환자에게 계속해서 말을 걸어 주세요.

_____ talking to the victim.

Answer Keep

21 응급처치를 할 수 있는 사람 계세요?

Is there anyone who can perform _____?

Answer first aid[emergency treatment]

22 그 환자분은 가스에 중독되었습니다.

The victim was _____ by gas.

Answer poisoned

23 감전사고가 발생하였습니다.

_____ has happened.

Answer An electric shock accident

24 **가스가 새는 것 같습니다.**

It seems that the gas is _____ .

Answer   leaking

25 **제 말 들리세요?**

Can you _____ me?

Answer   hear

26 **보호자는 있습니까?**

Do you have a _____ ?

Answer   guardian

27 **안심하세요.**

Don`t be _____ .

Don`t _____ .

Take it easy.

Answer   nervous/panic

28 **저의 지시에 따라주세요.**

Please _____ my instructions[directions].

Answer   follow

29 피가 멎을 때까지 솜으로 누르고 계세요.

_____ down with dried cotton until the bleeding stops.

Answer Press

30 나는 하임리크 구명법을 해 본적이 있다.

I have performed the Heimlich _____.

Answer maneuver

m / e / m / o

PART 03 구급(First Aid)

01 출산 예정이 언제입니까?

When is your baby _____ ?

When is your _____ date?

When is the _____ event?

When are you _____ your baby?

Answer   due/due/blessed/expecting

02 임신하신지 몇 개월입니까?

How long have you been _____ ?

Answer   pregnant[expecting]

03 가장 가까운 병원으로 데려다 주세요.

_____ me to the nearest hospital, please.

Answer   Take

04 평소에 지병이 있습니까?

Do you have a _____ at ordinary times?

Answer   chronic disease

05   진통은 몇 분 주기입니까?

How often do the _____ come?

Answer   labor pains

06   첫 출산이십니까?

Is this your first _____?

Answer   delivery

07   하혈이 있습니까?

Are you _____?

Are you discharging blood?

Do you have any bleeding?

Answer   bleeding

08   산모에게서 양수가 흘러나왔다.

Water _____ from the mother.

Water has broken from the mother.

Answer   broke

09   언제 증상이 처음 시작되었나요?

When did the _____ first occur?

Answer   symptom

10 목이 부었습니까?

Is your throat _____?

Answer swollen

11 손목을 삐셨나요?

Is your wrist _____?

Answer sprained

12 당신은 협심증에 관한 가족병력이 있습니까?

Do you have a _____ of angina?

Answer family history

13 몸에 열이 있나요?

Do you have a _____?

Answer fever

14 잠시만 숨을 참아주세요.

Please _____ your breath for a while.

Answer hold

15 그가 의식이 있습니까?

Is he _____?

Answer conscious

16 복용하고 있는 약이 있습니까?

Are there any medications you ?

Answer take

17 약물을 과다복용하셨나요?

Did you a medicine?

Answer overdose

18 목이 따가우십니까?

Do you have a throat?

Answer sore

19 구역질이 날 것 같습니까?

Are you ?

Do you feel nausea?

Answer nauseous

20 장애가 있습니까?

Do you have ?

Are you disabled?

Answer disability

21 그는 갑자기 쓰러졌습니다.

He suddenly _____.

He suddenly passed out.

He suddenly fell down.

Answer fainted

22 응급처치법을 알려 주세요.

Tell me how to perform _____.

Answer emergency treatment.

23 아이가 계속해서 토를 합니다.

My kid keeps _____.

My child keeps vomiting.

Answer throwing up

24 그의 몸에 경련이 일었다.

His whole body _____.

Answer convulsed

25 저는 당뇨 환자입니다.

I am a _____.

Answer diabetic

26 설사를 합니다.

I have

Answer diarrhea

27 저는 저혈압이 있습니다.

I have low

Answer blood pressure

28 배가 아픕니다.

My stomach   me.

I have a stomachache.

Answer pains

29 하임리크 구명법은 질식 시 가장 좋은 치료법이다.

The Heimlich maneuver is the best treatment for

Answer choking

30 맥박을 재겠습니다.

Let me   your pulse.

I'll take your pulse.

Answer check[feel]

31 급체인 듯합니다.

It seems that you are suffering from _____.

Answer   acute indigestion

32 가장 가까운 응급실로 가겠습니다.

We are going to the nearest _____.

Answer   emergency room

33 심폐소생술을 할 줄 아십니까?

Do you know how to perform[do] _____?

Answer   CPR(Cardiopulmonary Resuscitation)

m / e / m / o

01 이 지역은 오늘 저녁 태풍의 영향을 받게 됩니다.

This area will _____ the effect of the typhoon tonight.

Answer feel

02 생필품과 돈을 챙겨주시기 바랍니다.

Pack up some _____, please.

Answer necessities and money

03 갑자기 건물이 진동하였다.

The building suddenly _____.

Answer trembled

04 경주에 지진이 발생하였습니다.

There was an _____ in Gyeongju.

Answer earthquake

05 진도 6의 지진이 경주 지역을 강타했습니다.

An earthquake with a _____ of 6 hit the Gyeongju area.

Answer magnitude

06 **침수된 지역에서 자동차를 운전하지 마세요.**

Do not drive in any _____ areas.

Answer flooded[sunken]

07 **천둥 번개가 칠 경우는 건물 안으로 대피하세요.**

_____ into a building when there is lightning.

Answer Evacuate

08 **노약자와 어린이는 집 밖으로 나오지 못하게 하세요.**

Do not let _____ go out of the house.

Answer the elderly and children

09 **상수도 오염에 대비해서 욕조에 물을 받아 두세요.**

Fill up your bathtub with clean water in case of water

_____.

Answer pollution[contamination]

사고 유형별
필수 대화

사고 유형별 필수 영어 대화 문제

소방공무원을 위한
현장생활영어

PART 01 소방
(Fire Fighting)

○ 소방상식현황에 따라 긴급객출장치

1. 아파트 화재 관련 대화
(The Dialogue about an Apartment Fire)

신고(Report)

A: 119입니다. 무엇을 도와 드릴까요?

B: 불이 났어요!

A: 화재가 어디에 났나요, 선생님?

B: 방배동에 있는 롯데 캐슬 아파트에요.

A: 우선 진정하시구요. 아파트 몇 동 몇 호에서 불이 났습니까?

B: 107동이고요 몇 호 인지는 모르겠어요. 7층에서 불이 났어요.

A: 화재 규모가 어떻습니까, 선생님?

B: 불꽃은 보이지 않지만 연기가 많이 나요.

A: 알겠습니다. 실례지만 성함과 전화번호는 어떻게 되십니까?

B: 저는 ○○○이구요. 전화번호는 ○○○-○○○○-○○○○입니다.

A: 전화 주셔서 감사합니다. 소방차가 출동 중입니다. 대원들이 현장에 도착하면 전화를 할 테니까 전화를 받아 주시고 안내를 해 주시기 바랍니다.

A: This is 119. What can I do for you?

B: There is a fire!

A: Where is the fire, sir?

B: Lotte Castle Apartment in Bangbae-dong.

A: O.K. You need to calm down. What's the apartment number where the fire is located?

B: The building number is 107 but I don't know the apartment number. There is a fire on the seventh floor.

A: How large is the fire, sir?

B: I don't see flames but there is a lot of smoke.

A: O.K. Can I have your name and phone number, please?

B: I'm OOO and my phone number is OOO-OOO O-OOOO.

A: Thank you for your call. Fire engines are on their way and fire fighters will call you when they are at the scene. Please don't miss the call and show them the way, please.

2 신고(Report)

A: 119입니다. 무엇을 도와 드릴까요?

B: 시내에 있는 어떤 아파트에 큰 불이 났어요!

A: 정확하게 지금 어디에 계십니까?

B: 아, 몰라요! 초행길이라서.

A: 좋습니다. 주변에 눈에 띄는 큰 건물이 있습니까?

B: 네. 저 바로 앞에 국제무역센터 건물이 보입니다.

A: 좋습니다, 선생님. 성함이 어떻게 되시고 연락 가능한 번호가 어떻게 되세요?

B: 아. 저 이름은 ○○○입니다. 저 폰 번호는 ○○○-○○○○-○○○○입니다.

A: ○○○-○○○○-○○○○ 이 번호가 맞습니까?

B: 맞습니다.

A: 선생님, 도와 주셔서 감사합니다.

A: Hello. 119. What's your emergency?

B: There's a big fire in a downtown apartment!

A: What is your location exactly, please?

B: Gee, beats me!23) I am a stranger here.

A: O.K. Is there any landmark around you?

B: Yes, there is International Trade Center right in front of me.

A: All right, sir. Could I have your name and what number can I reach you?

B: Oh, my name is OOO. My phone number is OOO-OOOO-OOOO.

A: Is your number OOO-OOOO-OOOO, correct?

B: You've got it.

A: Thanks for your help, sir.

신고(Report)

A: 119입니다. 무엇을 도와 드릴까요?

B: 화재신고를 하려고요.

A: 어디서 불이 났나요, 선생님?

B: 서초동 무지개 아파트입니다. 연기가 많이 납니다.

A: 몇 층에서 불이 났습니까?

B: 5층인 듯합니다.

---

23) Beats me! = I don't know.

A: 알겠습니다. 우선 선생님이 진정하는 것이 중요합니다.

B: 알고 있습니다.

A: 지금 소방차를 가급적 빨리 출동시킬 테니, 전화를 끊지 마시고 우리가 도착하기 전에 계단을 이용해서 대피하여 주세요. 신고해 주셔서 고맙습니다.

A: Hello, this is 119. State your emergency, please.

B: I'd like to report a fire.

A: Where is the fire located, sir?

B: It is at Mujigae Apartment in Seocho-dong. There is a lot of smoke.

A: Which floor is on fire?[24]

B: It might be on the fifth floor.

A: I see. First of all, it is important for you to stay cool[calm].

B: I know.

A: A fire engine will be there as soon as possible. Please hold the line, take the stairs, and evacuate from the building before we get there. Thanks for your call.

2. 공장 화재 관련 대화

(The Dialogue about a Fire in a Factory)

신고(Report)

A: 안녕하세요, 방배소방서입니다. 무엇을 도와 드릴까요?

B: 공장에 불이 났어요! 빨리 와 주세요!

A: 선생님, 진정하시고요. 공장 이름이 무엇입니까? 혹시 주소를 아시나요?

B: 한국 제지 공장입니다. 주소는 갑자기 생각이 안나요.

A: 괜찮습니다. 공장 내부에 사람이 있는지 아십니까?

B: 모든 사람이 다 대피했습니다.

A: 공장 내부에 위험물이 있나요?

B: 전혀 모르겠습니다.

A: 그럼 불꽃이 보입니까?

B: 네. 큰 화염이 창문 밖으로 나오고 있고 3층에 많은 연기가 납니다. 빨리 좀 와 주세요!

A: 가급적 빨리 거기에 도착하겠습니다. 소방차를 보시면 안내 좀 부탁합니다. 신고해 주셔서 감사합니다.

---

24) What floor is the fire on?

A: Hello, Bangbae Fire Station. How can I help you?

B: There is a fire at the factory! Please hurry up!

A: Calm[Slow] down, sir. What is the name of the factory? Do you happen to know its address?

B: It is Korea Paper Factory. I suddenly have no idea about the address.

A: That's O.K. Do you know if there are people inside the factory?

B: Everyone has been evacuated.

A: Are there any dangerous materials inside the building?

B: I have no idea.

A: And then can you see the flames?

B: Yes, there are huge flames coming out of the windows and there's a lot of smoke on the third floor. Please hurry up!

A: O.K. We will be there as soon as possible. When you see the fire trucks, please show them the way.

공장 화재 현장에서

(At the scene of a factory fire)

A: 화재를 신고하신 분이 누구십니까?

B: 제가 했습니다.

A: 성함이 어떻게 되세요?

B: OOO입니다.

A: 그런데 이곳은 무슨 공장입니까?

B: 신발 공장입니다.

A: 공장 안에 아직도 사람이 있나요?

B: 아니요, 다행히 모두 퇴근했습니다.

A: 어디서 불이 처음 발생했나요?

B: 2층에서 연기가 나기 시작했습니다.

A: 화재 발생 시 비상벨이 울렸나요?

B: 네. 비상벨을 듣고 나서 건물에서 빠져나왔습니다.

A: 알겠습니다. 협조해 주셔서 감사합니다.

B: 별말씀을 다 하십니다.

A: Who is the one that reported the fire?

B: I did.

A: May I have your name, sir?

B: I am OOO.

A: By the way, what kind of factory is this?

B: It's a shoe factory.

A: Is anyone still inside the factory?

B: No, fortunately, every worker went home from work.

A: Where did the fire start?

B: The smoke came from the second floor.

A: Did the fire alarm go off when the fire started?

B: Yes, I evacuated from the building after I heard the fire alarm.

A: I see. Thank you for your cooperation.

B: It's my pleasure.

3. 산불 관련 대화
(The Dialogue about a Forest Fire)

신고(Report)

A: 관악소방서입니다. 무엇을 도와 드릴까요?

B: 여기 산불이 났어요! 도와주세요!

A: 자 진정하시고요. 불이 난 곳 위치가 어떻게 되나요?

B: 서울대학교 근처 관악산입니다.

A: 몇 부 능선에서 산불이 났는지 확인이 되시나요?

B: 정확히는 모르겠지만, 산중턱쯤인 것 같아요.

A: 연기가 많이 발생하나요?

B: 네.

A: 얼마나 멀리 불이 확산되고 있습니까?

B: 불길이 산 위로 빠르게 올라가고 있고 사방팔방으로 번지고 있습니다.

A: 알겠습니다. 지금 소방차가 출동 중에 있습니다. 소방차를 보시면 안내 좀 부탁드립니다. 신고해 주셔서 고맙습니다.

A: Gwanak Fire Department. What can I do for you, sir?

B: There is a bushfire! Help!

A: O.K. Keep yourself cool, please. Where is the location of the fire?

B: It is at Mt. Gwanak near Seoul National University.

A: Do you happen to know which part of the mountain is on fire?

B: Not exactly, but I guess it's in the middle of the mountain.

A: Do you see a lot of smoke?

B: Yes.

A: How far is the fire spreading?

B: The flames are rapidly making their way up to the mountain and spreading out in all directions.

A: O.K. Fire engines are on their way. When you see the fire engines, please show them the way. Thanks for your call.

m / e / m / o

PART 02 구조
(Rescue)

1. 교통사고 구조 관련 대화
(The Dialogue about Traffic Accident Rescue)

신고(Report)

A: 119입니다. 무엇을 도와 드릴까요?

B: 저에게 자동차 사고가 났어요!

A: 교통사고가 난 곳이 어디입니까?

B: 방배동 어디인데 정확히 어딘지는 잘 모르겠습니다.

A: 좋습니다. 선생님, 주변에 어떤 교통 표지판이 보입니까?
   아니면 근처에 큰 건물이 있는지요?

B: 저런! 방배경찰서가 제 앞에 있네요. 빨리 좀 와 주세요!

A: 알겠습니다. 구조대와 구급차를 지금 보내겠습니다.

A: This is 119. What's your emergency?

B: I have been in a car accident!

A: Where is the location of the traffic accident?

B: Somewhere in Bangbae-dong, but I don't know exactly where.

A: That's O.K. Sir, can you see any traffic signs around you? or are there any landmarks near you?

B: Gee! There is Bangbae Police Station in front of me. Hurry up, please!

A: I got it. We will send a rescue team with an ambulance right away.

🔳 신고(Report)

A: 관악소방서입니다. 무엇을 도와 드릴까요?

B: 교통사고가 났어요!

A: 사고 난 곳이 어디입니까?

B: 관악구청 근처입니다.

A: 네, 알겠습니다. 그런데 사고가 어떻게 났습니까?

B: 택시와 버스가 충돌했습니다.

A: 택시 안에 사람이 갇혀 있나요?

B: 모르겠는데요.

A: 알겠습니다. 신속히 신고해 주셔서 감사합니다. 구조대와 구급차가 지금 출동 중입니다.

A: Gwanak Fire Station. State your emergency, please.

B: There has been a car accident!

A: Where is the location of the accident?

B: It's around Gwanak-gu Office.

A: Yes, I've got it. By the way how did the accident occur?25)

B: A taxi collided with a bus.

A: Is there anyone stuck in the taxi?

B: You got me.26)

A: All right, sir. Thanks for your rapid report. Our rescue team with an ambulance is now on its way.

신고(Report)

A: 119입니다. 무엇을 도와 드릴까요?

B: 자동차 사고가 났습니다!

A: 사고 장소가 어디입니까, 선생님?

B: 서해안 고속도로입니다.

---

25) occur 대신에 happen, take place 등의 동사를 사용할 수 있다.

26) You got me. = Beats me! = You can search me. = Search me.

A: 그래요. 차 안에 갇혀 있는 분이 있나요 그리고 다친 사람은 없습니까?

B: 있어요. 3명이 차에서 나올 수가 없는데 한 사람은 출혈이 심합니다.

A: 알겠습니다. 어떻게 사고가 났습니까, 선생님?

B: 그게 그러니까 다중 충돌이었어요.

A: 선생님은 괜찮으세요?

B: 네, 현재로서는 전 괜찮습니다.

A: 알겠습니다, 선생님. 구조대와 구급차를 바로 보내드리겠습니다.

B: 감사합니다! 빨리 보내주세요!

A: 네, 그러겠습니다. 전화 주셔서 감사합니다.

A: 119. What's your emergency?

B: There's been a car accident!

A: What is your location, sir?

B: On the West Coast Expressway.

A: Thank you, sir. Is there anyone stuck in the car and is anyone hurt?

B: Yes, three people can't get out of the car and one of them is bleeding really badly.

A: OK. How did it happen, sir?

B: Well, it was a multiple collision.

A: Sir, are you OK?

B: Yes, as of now, I'm all right.[27]

A: All right, sir. We will send a rescue team and an ambulance right away.

B: Thanks! Please hurry up!

A: Yes, we will. Thank you for your call.

신고(Report)

A: 119입니다. 무엇을 도와 드릴까요, 선생님?

B: 자동차 사고가 났어요!

A: 사고 장소가 어디입니까, 선생님?

B: 서해 대교입니다.

A: 네, 다친 사람은 없습니까?

B: 제가 약간 부상을 입었고 제 친구 또한 다쳤습니다.

A: 알겠습니다. 어떻게 사고가 났습니까, 선생님?

B: 후유, 길이 미끄러워 차가 미끄러져 난간을 받았습니다.

A: 알겠습니다. 구조대와 구급차를 바로 보내겠습니다.

---

27) "As of now, I'm all right." 대신 "So far, so good."을 사용할 수 있다.

A: This is 119. How can I help you, sir?

B: There's been a car accident!

A: What's your location, sir?

B: I'm on Seohae Grand Bridge.

A: Okay, is anybody hurt[injured]?

B: I have a small injury and my friend is hurt, too.

A: I see, sir. How did the accident happen?

B: Well, the car skidded on the slippery road and hit a guardrail.

A: I got it. We will send a rescue team with an ambulance right away.

5 교통사고 현장에서(At the scene of a traffic accident)

A: 방배소방서 구급대원입니다. 사고가 어떻게 발생했는지 기억하십니까?

B: 자동차가 빗길에 미끄러져 가드레일에 부딪혔습니다.

A: 자, 경추보호대와 구출고정대를 착용할 테니 아프시면 말씀하세요.

B: 네.

A: 어느 병원에 가기를 원하십니까?

B: 가장 가까운 병원 응급실에 데려다 주세요.

A: 네, 그러겠습니다.

A: This is a paramedic from Bangbae Fire Department. Do you remember how the accident took place?

B: The car skidded in the rain and crashed into the guardrail.

A: Well, we will put a cervical collar and a KED[28] on you. Please tell me if it hurts.

B: Understood.

A: Which hospital do you want to go to?

B: Please bring me to the nearest[closest] emergency room[ER].

A: Yes, I will.

2. 산악사고 구조 관련 대화

(The Dialogue about Mountain Accident Rescue)

신고(Report)

A: 119입니다. 무엇을 도와 드릴까요?

---

28) 구출고정대 = KED(Kendrick Extrication Device)

B: 제 아내가 산에서 내려오다가 다쳤습니다. 움직이지 못하고 있어요!

A: 지금 계신 곳이 어디십니까, 선생님?

B: 관악산 정상 가까이에 있습니다.

A: 아내분이 어디를 다친 것 같습니까?

B: 발목을 삐어서 움직이질 못해요.

A: 알겠습니다. 구조팀이 도착할 때까지 아내분을 따뜻하게 해주시고 움직이지 않게 해주세요. 움직이면 상태가 악화될 수 있습니다.

B: 네, 어쨌든, 서둘러 주세요.

A: 네, 그러겠습니다!

A: This is 119. What's your emergency?

B: My wife got injured while walking down the mountain. She can't move!

A: What's your location, sir?

B: We are near the top of Mt. Gwanak.

A: Where do you think she was injured?

B: She sprained her ankle and can't move.

A: O.K., sir. Please keep her warm and still until the rescue team arrives. Moving might worsen the injury.

B: Okay, anyway, please hurry.

A: Yes, we will!

신고(Report)

A: 119입니다. 무엇을 도와 드릴까요, 선생님?

B: 제가 산을 오르다 다쳐서 움직이질 못해요. 헬리콥터가 필요해요.

A: 지금 계신 곳이 어디십니까, 선생님?

B: 지리산 천왕봉 정상 근처입니다.

A: 어디를 다치셨는지요?

B: 허리를 삔 것 같습니다.

A: 전화번호가 ○○○-○○○○-○○○○가 맞습니까?

B: 네, 맞습니다.

A: 구조대가 가면서 전화 드리면 안내 좀 해 주십시오.

B: 알겠습니다. 빨리 와 주세요.

A: 네, 선생님, 그렇게 하겠습니다.

A: This is 119. How can I help you, sir?

B: I got hurt while climbing up the mountain. I can't move. I need a chopper.

A: What's your location, sir?

B: It's near the top of Cheonwangbong on Mt. Jiri.

A: Where were you injured?

B: I guess I had my waist dislocated.

A: Is your phone number OOO-OOOO-OOOO, right?

B: Yes, that's correct.

A: Please guide the rescue team when they call you on their way.

B: I see. Make it haste, please.

A: Certainly, sir.

③ 산악사고 구조 현장에서

(At the scene of mountain accident rescue)

A: 119 구조대원입니다. 제 말 들리세요, 아주머니?

B: 네.

A: 어디가 가장 아프세요?

B: 오른발이 많이 아파요.

A: 많이 아프시더라도 잠시만 움직이지 마세요.

B: 네.

A: 우선 발목에 부목을 대고 들것으로 옮기겠습니다.

B: 살살 해 주세요. 너무 아파요.

A: 네, 그렇게요.

A: I am a 119 rescue worker. Can you hear me, ma'am?

B: Yes.

A: Where does it hurt most?

B: My right foot hurts a lot.

A: I know you are in a lot of pain, but remain still for a moment.

B: OK.

A: First, I will apply a splint to your ankle and carry you on a stretcher.

B: Do it gently, please. It hurts too much.

A: Yes, I will.

3. 수난사고 구조 관련 대화

(The Dialogue about Water Accident Rescue)

신고(Report)

A: 119입니다. 무엇을 도와 드릴까요?

B: 어떤 사람이 호수에 빠졌어요!

A: 지금 계신 곳이 어디십니까, 아주머니?

B: 모릅니다. 도와주세요. 제발, 어서요.

A: 얼마나 깊습니까?

B: 몰라요! 제발 빨리 오세요!

A: 자, 진정하시구요. 근처에 사람들이 있나요?

B: 아, 네. 한 사람 바꿔 줄게요. 그분한테 말씀하세요.

A: 좋습니다. 로프나 나뭇가지 같은 것을 물에 빠진 사람에게 던져주시고 물에는 들어가지 마세요.

B: 알겠습니다. 빨리 오세요.

A: This is 119. Please, state your emergency.

B: A certain person is drowning in a lake!

A: What's your location, ma'am?

B: I don't know. Help! Hurry, please!

A: How deep is it, ma'am?

B: Beats me! Please hurry!

A: Okay, calm down, please. Are there other persons around you?

B: Oh yes, I'll get one for you. Please talk to him.

A: All right. Throw a rope or a tree branch to the drowning person. Please do not go into the water.

B: Okay. Hurry up, please.

2 신고(Report)

A: 여보세요, 119입니다. 무엇을 도와 드릴까요?

B: 친구가 강에 빠졌어요!

A: 지금 계신 곳이 어딘가요?

B: 한강입니다.

A: 정확히 한강 어디쯤이죠?

B: 한강 선착장 바로 옆입니다.

A: 친구분이 보입니까?

B: 아니요, 커다란 물살에 휩쓸려 갔어요.

A: 구조대가 출동하였습니다. 로프나 나뭇가지 같은 것을 친구분에게 던져주시고 물에는 절대 들어가지 마세요.

B: 네. 제발 빨리 와주세요.

A: Hello, 119. What's your emergency?

B: My friend fell into a river!

A: Where are you now, sir?

B: We are at the Han River.

A: Where exactly are you at the Han River?

B: We are right next to the Han River dock.

A: Can you see your friend?

B: No, he was swept away in the strong current.

A: The rescue team was called out. Throw a rope or a tree branch to your friend and be sure not to go into the water.

B: O.K. Come quick, please.

4. 건설사고 구조 관련 대화
(The Dialogue about Construction Accident Rescue)

신고(Report)

A: 119입니다. 무엇을 도와 드릴까요?

B: 건설 현장 인부 한 명이 맨홀에 빠졌어요!

A: 위치가 어디입니까, 선생님?

B: 홍도 사거리에 있는 도로 건설 현장이에요.

A: 네, 그 맨홀 깊이가 어느 정도 됩니까?

B: 정확하게는 모르지만 깊이가 대략 7미터 정도 됩니다.

A: 즉시 구조팀을 보내드리겠습니다.

B: 고맙습니다!

A: This is 119. Please state your emergency.

B: A construction worker fell into a manhole!

A: What is your location, sir?

B: It's at a road construction site in the Hongdo crossroads[intersection].

A: OK, how deep is the manhole?

B: I am not sure but it looks[seems] like about 7 meters deep

A: We will send a rescue team right away.

B: Thanks a lot!

신고(Report)

A: 관악소방서입니다. 무엇을 도와 드릴까요?

B: 아이가 맨홀에 빠졌어요!

A: 맨홀이 있는 위치가 어디입니까?

B: 동부 센트레빌 아파트 근처 도로공사 현장입니다.

A: 혹시 맨홀 깊이가 어느 정도 되는지 아십니까?

B: 9~10미터 정도 되는 것 같아요.

A: 그 아이 의식이 있어 보이나요?

B: 네. 의식이 있는 것 같아요.

A: 지금 즉시 출동하겠습니다.

B: 알겠습니다!

A: Gwanak Fire Station. What can I do for you, sir?

B: A kid fell into a manhole!

A: Where is the manhole located?

B: It is at a road construction site around Dongbu Centreville Apartment.

A: Do you happen to know how deep the manhole is?

B: I guess it's 9 or 10 meters deep.

A: Does the kid look conscious?

B: Yes. He/She seems[appears] conscious.

A: We will dispatch our rescue team.

B: O.K.!

신고(Report)

A: 119입니다. 무엇을 도와 드릴까요?

B: 여기서 건설 중인 건물이 무너져 내렸어요!

A: 위치가 어디입니까?

B: 잘 모르겠는데요. 현장 주임을 바꿔 드리겠으니 이 사람에게 물어보세요.

A: 네, 고맙습니다. 그리고 의식을 잃지 않도록 사고를 당한 분들에게는 계속해서 말을 걸어 주세요.

B: 네, 그럴게요.

A: 119. What's your emergency?

B: A building under construction has collapsed over here!

A: What's your location, please?

B: I don't know. I will get you my foreman, and you could ask him.

A: Yes, thank you, sir. And please keep talking to the victims in order for them not to lose their senses[consciousness].

B: Yes, I will.

건설사고 구조 현장에서
(At the scene of construction accident rescue)

A: 구조대원입니다. 선생님, 제 말 들리세요?

B: 네, 하지만 다리가 아프고 여기 공간이 너무 좁아 움직일 수가 없어요.

A: 그러면 손은 사용할 수 있으세요?

B: 아니요, 못해요.

A: 괜찮습니다, 당황하지 마세요. 구조대원들이 지금 내려갑니다.

B: 네, 제발 서둘러 주세요.

A: 우선 다리에 부목을 댄 후 들것으로 옮기겠습니다. 아프더라도 참으세요. 얼마 걸리지 않을 겁니다.

B: 네.

A: This is a rescuer. Can you hear me, sir?

B: Yes, but my legs hurt and the space here is too small for me to move.

A: And then can you use your hands?

B: No, I can't.

A: That's OK, don't panic. Rescuers are now coming down.

B: Okay, please hurry up.

A: First of all, we will apply a splint to your legs and then carry you on a stretcher. Even if it hurts, please be patient. It won't take long.

B: O.K.

⑤ 건설사고 구조 현장에서

(At the scene of construction accident rescue)

A: 사고가 어떻게 발생했는지 설명해 줄 수 있겠습니까?

B: 네. 사다리를 올라가고 있었어요. 사다리 꼭대기까지 올라

갔을 때 갑자기 미끄러져 떨어졌어요.

A: 가장 아픈 곳이 어디입니까?

B: 머리, 골반, 오른쪽 허벅지가 아파요.

A: 오른쪽 다리를 올려 보세요.

B: 아이고! 아파라!

A: 여기도 아픈가요?

B: 예!

A: 여기에 감각 있습니까?

B: 예.

A: 좋아요! 움직이지 마세요. 구출고정대와 부목을 착용시키 겠습니다. 혹시 마음에 두고 있는 특별한 병원이라도 있습 니까?

B: 아니요, 없습니다.

A: 그렇다면 가장 가까운 응급실로 모셔다 드리겠습니다. 괜찮 습니까?

B: 좋습니다.

A: Can you explain how the accident happened?

B: Yes. I was climbing up a ladder. When I reached the top of it, I suddenly slipped and fell down.

A: What's troubling you most?

B: I feel pain in my head, hip, and right thigh.

A: Raise your right leg, please.

B: Ouch! It hurts!

A: Do you pain here, too?

B: Yes!

A: Do you have a sense here?

B: Yes.

A: OK! Don't move. I will secure you in a KED and a splint. Is there any particular hospital in your mind?[29]

B: No, there isn't.

A: Then, we will take you to the nearest emergency room, all right?

B: OK.

5. 승강기사고 구조 관련 대화

(The Dialogue about Elevator Accident Rescue)

신고(Report)

A: 119입니다. 무엇을 도와 드릴까요?

---

29) 유사표현인 "다니시는 병원이 있습니까?"는 "Do you have a regular hospital that you usually go to."라고 한다.

B: 승강기 안에 제가 갇혔어요!

A: 혼자 갇히신 겁니까, 선생님?

B: 네, 경비실에 연락을 해보았지만 인터콤이 고장 났어요.

A: 아주머니, 현재 위치가 어디인가요?

B: 대치동 타워 팰리스 210동 1라인입니다.

A: 네, 지금 구조대원들은 출동시킬 테니 안심하고 잠시만 기다려 주세요.

B: 고맙습니다.

A: This is 119. What's your emergency?

B: I am stuck in the elevator!

A: Are you alone there, sir?

B: Yes, I tried to contact the superintendent's office, but the intercom was out of order.

A: What is your current location, ma'am?

B: It's Tower Palace in Daechi-dong. Line 1 in Building No. 210.

A: OK, don't worry. The rescue team will be there soon. Please remain calm and wait a minute.

B: Thanks a lot.

2 승강기 사고 구조 현장에서

(At the scene of elevator accident rescue)

A: 구조대원입니다. 자 안심하시고 잠시만 기다리세요.

B: 네, 무서워요. 빨리 꺼내 주세요.

A: 거기에 몇 분이 계세요?30)

B: 저 혼자입니다. 제발 서둘러 주세요!

A: 네, 당황하지 마시고 제 지시를 따라 주세요.

B: 예.

A: 우선, 안쪽에서 문을 벌려 보세요. 제 말 듣고 계시죠?31)

B: 네, 말씀대로 했어요.

A: 한 발짝 떨어지십시오. 우리가 문을 열겠습니다.

B: 네.

A: I am a member of the rescue team. Please don't be nervous and wait a second.

B: OK, I am so scared. Please take me out as soon as possible.

A: How many people are there (in the elevator)?

B: I am just alone. Make it haste, please!

---

30) "일행이 몇 분 되세요?"라고 할 경우에는 "How many in your company?"라고 하면 되겠다.
31) "제 말이 들립니까?"는 "Can you hear me?"라고 한다.

A: Okay, please don't panic and follow my directions.

B: Yes.

A: First of all, try to open the door inside. Are you listening to me?

B: Yes, I have done what you said.

A: Step away from the door. We are going to open the door.

B: Sure.

6. 공장사고 구조 관련 대화
(The Dialogue about Factory Accident Rescue)

신고(Report)

A: 119입니다. 무엇을 도와 드릴까요?

B: 구조대를 급히 보내주세요! 프레스에 어떤 사람의 왼손이 끼었어요!

A: 침착하시구요. 기계전원은 차단했습니까?

B: 네, 이미 껐어요.

A: 잘하셨습니다! 위치가 어떻게 되세요?

B: 부천 공단 2블록에 위치한 ○○ 방직 공장입니다.

A: 선생님, 환자의 상태는 어떻습니까?

B: 의식은 있는데, 출혈이 심합니다.

A: 선생님, 그러면 지혈32)을 계속 해주시고 환자가 의식을 잃
지 않도록 계속 말을 걸어 주세요.

B: 네, 그럴게요.

A: 감사합니다. 구조대가 곧 현장에 도착할 겁니다.

A: 119. What's your emergency?

B: Please dispatch a rescue team! Someone's left
hand got stuck in the presser!

A: Calm down, please. Did you turn off the power
of the machine?

B: Yes, I already did.

A: Attaboy! What's your location?

B: This is ○○ Textile Factory in Block 2 in Bucheon
Industrial Complex.

A: Sir, please describe the condition of the patient.

B: He is conscious, but he is bleeding too much.

A: And then, sir, maintain hemostasis and keep talking to the victim in order for him not to lose his
consciousness.

B: Yes, I will.

---

32) 지혈하다 = arrest[check, stanch, staunch, stem, stop] the bleeding

A: Thank you, sir. Our rescue team will be there soon.

공장사고 구조 현장에서

(At the scene of factory accident rescue)

A: 선생님이 이 사건을 신고하셨나요?

B: 네, 제가 신고했습니다.

A: 잘하셨습니다. 전원은 차단하셨나요?

B: 네, 즉시 차단했어요.

A: 아주 잘하셨습니다. 계속 지혈을 해주세요.

B: 네.

A: 이 기계를 잘 아시는 분이 계시는지요?

B: 저도 이 기계에 대해 잘 알고 있습니다.

A: 잘되었네요! 당황하지 마시고 제 지시를 따라 주세요.

B: 네, 그럴게요.

A: Sir, did you report the accident?

B: Yes, I did.

A: Good job. Did you turn off the power of the machine?

B: Yes, I turned it off immediately.

A: You did a great job. Please continue to stop the bleeding.

B: Yes.

A: Is there anyone who knows this machine well?

B: I'm familiar with the machine, too.

A: Good for you! Please don't panic and follow my instructions.

B: Yes, I will.

m / e / m / o

PART 03 구급 · 응급 치료
(First Aid)

1. 심폐소생술 관련 대화
(The Dialogue about Cardiopulmonary Resuscitation)

신고(Report)

A: 119입니다. 무엇을 도와 드릴까요?

B: 어르신 한 분이 가슴을 움켜쥔 채 바닥에 쓰러졌어요!

A: 장소가 어딥니까?

B: 메가박스 코엑스입니다.

A: 환자 의식은 있습니까?

B: 아니오. 의식이 없습니다.

A: 호흡은 하고 있습니까?

B: 아니요, 숨도 안 쉬고 심장도 뛰지 않아요.

A: 혹시 심폐소생술을 할 줄 아세요?

B: 아니요.

A: 그러면 전화를 받으면서 지시에 따르세요.

B: 네.

A: 선생님 손바닥 중앙을 환자의 양쪽 젖꼭지 사이의 흉부의 정중앙에 놓고 선생님 손가락이 환자의 늑골에 닿지 않도록 하세요.

B: 네.

A: 다른 손으로 나머지 손을 덮어주세요. 그리고 팔을 쭉 펴고 수직으로 약 5~6cm 정도 환자 가슴을 눌러 준 다음 힘을 뺍니다.

B: 네.

A: 분당 100회의 속도로 30회 환자의 흉부를 압박합니다. 흉부압박 시 환자의 가슴에서 선생님의 양손을 떼지 마세요.

B: 네.

A: 매 30회 흉부압박이 끝날 때마다 구조 호흡을 두 번 실행합니다. 환자의 머리를 뒤로 젖히고, 기도를 열어준 다음 환자의 코를 꼭 집고 시행합니다. 환자의 호흡이나 기침 또는 움직임이 있을 때에는 즉시 흉부압박을 중지하고 호흡을 확인해 주세요. 호흡이 없으면 환자가 스스로 호흡을 할 때까지 CPR을 계속합니다.

B: 말씀하신 대로 하고 있습니다.

A: 감사합니다.

A: 119. State your emergency.

B: A certain senile fell down to the floor, holding his heart in his hands!

A: What is your location?

B: Megabox COEX.

A: Is the patient conscious?

B: No, he is unconscious.

A: Is he breathing?

B: No, he stopped breathing and his heart has stopped.

A: Do you happen to know how to do CPR[33])?

B: No, I don't.

A: OK, then, please follow my directions while answering the phone.

B: Yes.

A: Place the palm of your hand in the center of the patient's chest between the nipples. Do not let your hand touch the patient's ribs.

B: O.K.

A: Place one of your hands on top of the other hand, stretch out your arms, push straight down to compress the victim's chest at a depth of about 5~ 6cm, and then stop applying pressure.

B: Okay.

A: Perform 30 chest compressions on the victim at the rate of 100 times per minute. Do not keep your hands off the victim's chest during the procedure.

B: O.K.

A: Every time you complete 30 chest compressions on the victim, administer two rescue breaths with the victim's head tilted back, to open the airway, and the victim's nose pinched.

B: OK.

A: When the victim starts to breathe, cough, or move, stop chest compressions on him immediately and monitor his breathing. Unless the victim is breathing, continue doing CPR on him until the victim is breathing on his own.

B: I am just following your instructions.

A: Thank you, sir.

---

33) CPR = Cardiopulmonary Resuscitation(심폐소생술)

2. 협심증 관련 대화

(The Dialogue about Angina)

신고(Report)

A: 관악소방서입니다.

B: 아빠가 아파요! 도와주세요!

A: 그래, 얘야, 우선 침착하고! 집이 어디니?

B: 관악구 은천로 33길 5입니다.

A: 아이고 똑똑해라! 그래, 아빠가 어디가 아프데요?

B: 가슴이 아프다고 해요.

A: 왼쪽 팔과 등 쪽은?

B: 네, 많이 아프데요.

A: 옛날에도 아프다고 하셨어?

B: 2주 전에도 협심증으로 입원했어요.

A: 그랬어? 근데 아빠가 약은 먹어요?

B: 네, 어떤 알약을 드세요.

A: 그랬구나. 그럼 그 약을 아빠 혀 밑으로 넣을래요?

B: 네, 알겠습니다.

A: Gwanak Fire Station.

B: Daddy is sick! Help me!

A: OK, kid, for now, be cool! And where is your house located?

B: It's Road no. 33-5, Euncheon-ro, Gwanak-gu.

A: So smart you are! And then, what's wrong with Daddy?

B: He says he has a pain in his chest.

A: Does he feel pain radiating from his left arm to his back?

B: Yes, he says he feels a lot of pain.

A: Has he ever felt this pain in the past?

B: He was also hospitalized with angina two weeks ago.

A: Oh, was he? By the way, does Daddy take any medication for this?

B: Yes, he does. He takes a certain pill.

A: So he does. OK, please put that tablet under Daddy's tongue.

B: OK, I got it.

3. 심장마비 관련 대화
(The Dialogue about Heart Attack)

신고(Report)

A: 119입니다. 무엇을 도와 드릴까요?

B: 저 여자 친구가 갑자기 쓰러졌어요! 기절한 것 같아요!34)

A: 진정하시구요. 위치가 어디세요?

B: 방배역 3번 출구입니다.

A: 여자 친구분이 숨은 쉬나요?

B: 네. 신음은 하지만 눈을 뜨지 못해요.

A: 네. 구급차는 지금 출동했고요 구급대원들이 현장으로 가면
서 전화를 할 겁니다.

B: 알겠습니다. 빨리 와 주세요.

A: This is 119. What is the problem with you?

B: My female friend suddenly fell down to the
ground! She seems to pass out!

A: Please calm down. Where are you?

B: We are in front of Exit 3 of Bangbae Station.

---

34) 기절하다 = black out, faint, swoon
혼수상태이다 = be in lethargy
혼수상태에 빠지다 = fall into a coma

A: Is she breathing?

B: Yes. She is moaning but she feels uneasy to open her eyes.

A: I see. The ambulance has just left and our paramedics will call you on their way to the scene.

B: I see. Hurry up, please.

4. 임산부 관련 대화
(The Dialogue about a Pregnant Woman)

신고(Report)

A: 119입니다. 무엇을 도와 드릴까요?

B: 임산부인데 배가 너무 아파요!35)

A: 주소가 어떻게 되세요?

B: 서초구 방배동 효령로 33-5번지입니다. 빨리 좀 와주세요.

A: 출산 예정일이 언제입니까?36)

B: 다음 주요.

A: 양수가 터졌나요?

B: 네.

---

35) 진통은 labor pains라고 하며 복통은 colic 또는 bellyache라고 한다.

36) 동일한 표현으로 "When is your due date?", "When is the blessed event?", "When are you expecting your baby?" 등이 있다. 참고로 "임신한지 얼마나 되었습니까?"라고 할 때 는 "How long have you been pregnant?"라고 한다.

A: 하혈은요?

B: 네.

A: 알겠습니다. 바로 구급차를 보내드리겠습니다.

B: 고맙습니다.

A: 119. How can I help you?

B: I am pregnant[37] and in terrible pain!

A: What's your address, ma'am?

B: I am at 33-5, Hyoryeong-ro, Banbae-dong, Seocho-gu. Hurry, please.

A: When is your baby due, ma'am?

B: Next week.

A: Has your water broken?

B: Yes.

A: Are you discharging blood (from your vagina)?[38]

B: Yes.

A: O.K. We will send you an ambulance immediately.

B: Thanks a lot.

---

37) "I am expecting."이라고도 한다.

38) 하혈이 있습니까? = Are you bleeding? = Do you have any bleeding?

임산부 이송 현장에서

(At the scene of transporting a pregnant woman)

A: 어느 병원으로 갈까요?

B: 오산당병원으로 가고 싶습니다.

A: 출산 예정일이 언제입니까?

B: 다음 주입니다.

A: 언제 진통이 시작되었습니까?[39]

B: 2시간 전에 시작되었습니다.

A: 이번이 첫 출산이십니까?

B: 아닙니다. 두 번째입니다. 입덧도 심하게 해 본적이 없어요.

A: 그러면, 진통이 더 짧겠네요. 자궁 수축 간격이 어느 정도 걸립니까?

B: 약 2분 정도이구요 진통이 왔다 갔다 합니다.

A: 하혈이 있거나 양수가 흘렀습니까?

B: 잘 모르겠습니다.

A: 그러면 확인하겠습니다.

B: 네, 그러시죠.

---

39) 참고로 "마지막 생리는 언제 했나요?"는 "When was your last period?"라고 한다.

A: Which hospital do you want to go to, ma'am?

B: I would like to go to Osandang Hospital.

A: When is your baby due, ma'am?

B: Next week.

A: When did the labor pains first start?

B: They started two hours ago.

A: Is this your first delivery?

B: No, this is the second time for me. I have never suffered greatly from morning sickness.

A: OK, then your labor should be shorter. How long does it take between each contraction?

B: About every two minutes and the pains come and go.

A: Do you have any bleeding? Or has your water[40] broken?

B: I don't know exactly.

A: Let me check, then.

B: Sure.

---

40) 이 경우의 water는 양수의 의미로 의학적 용어로는 amniotic fluid라고 한다.

5. 영유아 관련 대화

(The Dialogue about Infants)

신고(Report)

A: 119입니다. 무엇을 도와 드릴까요?

B: 우리 아기가 열이 나고 숨을 잘 못 쉽니다.

A: 아기가 몇 살이죠?

B: 2개월입니다.

A: 혹시 아기 눈이 돌아가거나 몸이 경직되었습니까?

B: 아니요.

A: 알겠습니다. 주소는요, 어머니?

B: 서초구 방배 3동 159번지입니다.

A: 알겠습니다. 구급차가 지금 주소지로 가고 있습니다.

B: 도와주셔서 정말 감사합니다.

A: This is 119. What can I do for you?

B: My baby has a high fever and can't breathe well.

A: How old is the baby?

B: 2 months.[41]

A: Are the baby's eyes turned up or to the side? Or
has the baby's body stiffened?

B: No.

A: OK. Can I get your address, mam?

B: I am at 159, Bangbae 3-dong, Seocho-gu.

A: Okay. The ambulance is on its way to your address.

B: I really appreciate your help.

신고(Report)

A: 방배소방서입니다. 무엇을 도와 드릴까요?

B: 제 아이가 계속 구토를 하고 몸이 경직되었어요. 도와주세요!

A: 침착하시구요. 주소는요?

B: 서초구 방배 1동 981-1번지입니다.

A: 알겠습니다. 아이가 몇 살이죠?

B: 3살입니다.

A: 우선 미지근한 물로 아이 몸을 깨끗한 수건으로 닦아 주고 계세요. 구급대원과 구급차를 속히 보내도록 하겠습니다.

B: 알겠습니다.

---

41) "It is 2 months old."를 줄여서 사용한 문장이다. 성별을 구별하는 의미가 없을 때는 사람에게도 대명사 it을 사용할 수 있다.

A: Bangbae Fire Department. What's your emergency?

B: My child keeps vomiting and his body is stiff. Help, please!

A: Be cool! And your address, please?

B: 981-1, Bangbae 1-dong, Seocho-gu.

A: Okay, how old is your kid?

B: (He is) 3 years old.

A: First, please wash the kid's body with lukewarm water, using a clean towel. We will dispatch our paramedics with an ambulance.

B: I got it.

6. 화상 관련 대화
(The Dialogue about Burns)

신고(Report)

A: 119입니다. 무엇을 도와 드릴까요?

B: 우리 애가 화상을 입었어요! 빨리 와 주세요!

A: 어머니, 침착하시구요. 아이가 언제 화상을 입었습니까?

B: 약 10분 전에요.

A: 어쩌다 화상을 입었습니까?

B: 끓고 있는 국에 화상을 입었어요.

A: 어느 부위에 화상을 입었나요?

B: 왼팔이요.

A: 주소가 어떻게 되세요, 어머님?

B: 부천시 소사구 원미동 11-1번지입니다.

A: 일단 화상을 입은 표피를 흐르는 물에다 데시고 식혀주세요.

B: 네.

A: 구급대원과 구급차가 지금 주소지로 가고 있습니다.

B: 네, 기다리고 있겠습니다. 고맙습니다.

A: 119. What's your emergency?

B: My kid got burned! Come quick, please!

A: Ma'am, stay calm, please. When did your child get burned?

B: Around 10 minutes ago.

A: How did he burn himself?

B: He burned himself from boiling soup.

A: What part of the body was burned?

B: His left arm.

A: What is your address, ma'am?

B: I am at 11-1, Wonmi-dong, Sosa-gu, Bucheon-si.

A: For the present, cool the surface of the burnt skin with running water.

B: Okay.

A: The paramedics with an ambulance are now on their way to your address.

B: Yes, I will be waiting for them. Thank you.

② 화상환자 이송 현장에서
(At the scene of transporting a burn victim)

A: 언제 아이가 화상을 당했습니까?

B: 15분 전에요.

A: 어떻게 화상을 당했나요?

B: 폭죽을 가지고 놀다가요.

A: 어디에 화상을 입었나요?

B: 오른쪽 다리입니다.

A: 가위로 아이의 옷을 찢겠습니다. 괜찮습니까?

B: 네.

A: 어느 병원으로 갈까요?

B: 화상치료가 가능한 병원이면 어느 곳이나 좋습니다.

A: 가장 가까운 화상치료 센터는 강남성모병원입니다. 거기로 모셔다 드릴까요?

B: 네, 빨리 가 주세요.

A: When did your child get burned?

B: 15 minutes ago.

A: How did she get burned?

B: From firecrackers she played with.

A: What part of the body was burned?

B: Her right leg.

A: I will remove the kid's clothes with scissors. Is it OK?

B: Okay.

A: What hospital do you want to go to?

B: Whatever hospital would be OK where burn treatments are available.

A: The closest burn center is Gangnam St. Mary's Hospital. Do you want us to take you there?

B: Yes, hurry, please.

7. 복통 관련 대화
(The Dialogue about Stomachaches)

신고(Report)

A: 119입니다. 어떤 상황인가요?

B: 배가 너무 아파요! 좀 도와주세요!

A: 네. 언제부터 아프셨어요?

B: 30분 전쯤이요.

A: 설사를 하셨습니까? 토하실 것 같은가요?42)

B: 네. 설사도 하고 속도 울렁거립니다.

A: 마지막 식사 때 무엇을 드셨어요?

B: 오늘 점심으로 피자를 4판이나 먹었어요. 저 생각엔 급체인 것 같아요.

A: 그래요? 그러면 소화제 가지고 계십니까?

B: 네.

A: 그러면 소화제 2알을 드시고 안정을 취하세요.

B: 네, 그렇게 할게요. 알려주셔서 고맙습니다.

---

42) 유사표현인 "어지러움을 느끼세요?"는 "Do you feel dizzy?"라고 한다.

A: This is 119. What's your situation?

B: I feel a sharp pain in the stomach! Please help me!

A: O.K. When did it start?

B: About half an hour ago.

A: Did you have diarrhea? Do you feel nauseous?

B: Yes, both.

A: What did you have for your last meal?

B: I'd 4 pizzas for lunch today. I guess I am suffering from acute indigestion.

A: You did? Well, do you have anything for digestion?

B: Yes.

A: And then, take two pills and relax yourself.

B: Yes, I will. Thank you for your tip.

복통환자 이송 현장에서

(At the scene of transporting a stomachache victim)

A: 어디가 가장 아프세요?

B: 배가 너무 쑤시는 것처럼 아파요.

A: 언제부터 증상이 시작되었나요?

B: 20분 전쯤입니다.

A: 배를 한 번 만져볼게요. 아프면 말씀하세요.

B: 그만, 너무 아파요.

A: 창백해 보입니다. 저녁식사로 무엇을 드셨나요?

B: 갈치회를 몇 점 먹었습니다. 급성 장염인 것 같습니다.

A: 네, 그러면 가까운 병원에 모셔다 드리겠습니다.

B: 네, 그렇게 하세요.

A: Where does it hurt most, sir?[43]

B: I have an acute stomachache.[44]

A: When did the symptom first occur?

B: It started around 20 minutes ago.

A: Let me press your stomach. Tell me if it hurts.

B: Stop! It hurts hard!

A: You look pale. What did you eat for dinner?

B: I ate some slices of raw hairtail.[45] It seems to me
   I suffer from acute enteritis.

A: OK, then we will take you to the nearest hospital.

B: Yes, as you like it.

---

43) 동일한 표현으로 "Where do you have the most pain?"이 있다.

44) 유사표현인 "칼로 콕콕 찌르듯 아프다."는 "I have a stabbing pain in the stomach."라고
한다.

45) hairtail = cutlassfish(갈치)

Ⅲ 사고 유형별 필수 영어 대화 문제

※ 다음 대화의 흐름으로 보아 빈칸에 들어갈 가장 적절한 것을 고르시오. [1~14]

01

A: This 119. What's your emergency?

B: There might be a tsunami. What should I do?

A: What's your current location?

B: 4567 Banpo-dong

A: You are in a tsunami danger zone. Pack simple neces-
saries and prepare to evacuate.

B: OK, but where should I evacuate to?

A: (   )

① Evacuate to a higher place if the water level keeps rising.

② Avoid dangerous areas and only use safe roads.

③ There is a shelter at Banpo High School.

④ Seoul areas are under a typhoon threat.

Answer ③

02

A: Is anybody there?

B: Yes, here.

A: I'm a rescue worker from Banpo Fire Station. Can you
hear me?

B: Yes.

A: (   )

B: There are five people here and one person is unconscious.

① Do you have any friends or relatives you can stay with?

② What kind of fire escape equipment is installed in the building?

③ Did you hear any explosions or other strange sounds?

④ Can you tell me about your current situation there?

Answer ④

03

A: Who is the owner of this car?

B: It belongs to me.

A: (   )

B: I heard the alarm sounds and it was on fire.

① Do you know the cause of the fire?

② Do you know the year of the car?

③ How did you know there was a fire?

④ Who set off the fire alarm?

Answer ③

04

A: How many stories are there in this edifice?

B: There are 3 basements and the structure is twelve stories high.

A: (   )

B: We have one main stairway and one escape stairway.

① How many stairs are there in this building?

② Are there any multipurpose facilities in this building?

③ How did you know there was a fire?

④ Does the fire extinguishing equipment work properly?

Answer ①

05

A: For now, you need to soothe yourself. What is the apartment number where the fire is found?

B: It's Building 106, and the fire started at the ninth or tenth floor.

A: (   )

B: I don't see flames but there is a lot of smoke.

① Where is the location of the fire?

② What's your emergency?

③ Do you see flames or smoke?

④ Are there any Koreans around you?

Answer ③

06

A: What's your location?

B: Seobong Industry in Gimpo-si, Gyeonggi-do.

A: Is she injured a lot?

B: (   )

① I don't know, but she is in great pain.

② I am pregnant and I am in terrible pain.

③ Find out if there is a medicine bottle near the victim.

④ I am not sure, but I guess she is on the fence.

Answer ①

07

A: 119. How can I help you, sir?

B: A construction worker fell (ⓐ) a manhole!

A: OK, how (ⓑ) is the manhole?

B: It seems like around 7 meters.

① into/high

② into/deep

③ in/high

④ in/deep

Answer ②

08

A: Excuse me. I'm looking for Nambu Bus Terminal.

B: Ah, it's right over there.

A: Come again? (   )

B: OK. Just walk down the street, and then turn left at the first intersection. It's on your left. You can't miss it.

① Do you think I am punctual?

② Will you do me a favor?

③ Could you be more specific?

④ Will you run right into it?

Answer ③

09

A: Mom, my stomach (   )

B: Do you (   ) a fever?

A: No, I don't think so.

B: Do you (   ) nauseous?

A: No, not at all. But you know, I did have potato chips and peanut butter for today's lunch.

B: So you did.

① has/feel/hurt   ② hurts/have/feel

③ hurts/feel/have   ④ feels/have/hurt

Answer ②

10

A: Did you see Mr. Lee this morning?

B: Yes. But whey does he (   )?

A: I have no idea.

B: I thought he'd be happy.

A: Me too. Especially since he got promoted last week.

B: He may have some problems with his female friend.

① have such a long face

② jump on the bandwagon

③ play a good hand

④ step into my shoes   Answer ①

11

A: Frankly speaking, I don't think my new boss knows what he is doing.

B: He is young, Buddy. You have to give him a chance.

A: How many chances do I have to give him? He's really nuts!

B: (   )

A: What? Where?

B: Over there.

① Speak of the devil.

② Keep up the good work.

③ Money makes the mare go.

④ I wish you good luck.   Answer ①

12

A: Hello, Susan.

B: Hello, Brad. Are you and Martha free this Saturday?

A: Saturday? She would go shopping, but I am not sure. Why do you ask?

B: I thought I would invite you guys to dinner.

A: Well, let me check it again with her and give you a ring this evening.

B: Sounds great! (   )

① How could you stand me up like this?

② Thank you for having me, Buddy.

③ You should have made it on time.

④ I'll be waiting for your call.   Answer ④

13

A: He was hit by a drunk driver.

B: How old was the driver?

A: He was only seventeen. (   ). He had been drinking at a local bar.

B: Gosh! Is there any possibility that he is free from D.W.I.?

① He took that with a grain of salt

② He hit the jackpot

③ He was under the influence

④ He is with you on this one   Answer ③

14

A: You know, I'm getting transferred to Spain.

B: Spain? Is that good or bad?

A: Oh, I've been hoping for it.

B: (   )

① I really wanted to go to Spain.

② I appreciate your patience.

③ In that case, I'm happy for you.

④ Oh, that's not easy for me.

Answer ③

※ 다음 대화를 읽고 물음에 답하시오. [15~16]

A: What're your symptoms?

B: I feel a stabbing pain in the stomach.

A: Let me press your stomach. Tell me if it hurts.

B: OK.

A: Do you feel pain here?

B: Oops! It hurts badly.

A: Can you lift your left leg up to your stomach?

B: No, impossible.

A: Well, it seems to me that you have acute (ⓐ). We'll take you to the nearest hospital.

B: Please do so.

15 A와 B의 관계를 가장 잘 설명한 것은?

① teacher : student   ② doctor : patient

③ rescue worker : victim   ④ clerk : guest

Answer ③

16 ⓐ에 들어갈 말로 가장 적당한 것은?

① knowledge   ② hearing

③ sense   ④ enteritis

Answer ④

17 다음 두 사람이 대화하고 있는 장소로 가장 적절한 곳을 고르시오.

A: Hurry up! She's unconscious.

B: Bring her over here to the bed. What happened?

A: She was in a traffic accident twenty minutes ago. She got hit by a car while she was crossing the street.

B: What kind of first aid have you given the victim on the way here?

A: Well, I secured her neck and tried to stop the bleeding.

B: All right. We'll take over from here.

① emergency room

② daycare center

③ post office

④ convenience store

Answer ①

18 다음 밑줄 친 부분과 가장 가까운 뜻은?

> A: Why do you have to be so stubborn?
> B: I don't know. That's just the way I am. I guess <u>I'm just a chip off[of] the old block.</u>

① I'm just like my father.

② I'm just in a bad mood.

③ I just have confidence in my intuition.

④ I just like to have fun with old friends.

Answer ①

※ 대화의 빈칸에 들어갈 말로 가장 적절한 것을 고르시오. [19~20]

19

> A: Would you like to get some coffee?
> B: That's an excellent idea.
> A: Should we buy an Americano or a Cafe-Latte?
> B: It doesn't matter to me. (   )
> A: I think I will get an iced Americano.
> B: It's a good choice!

① Not really.

② Suit yourself.

③ Maybe just a handful or so.

④ Come see for yourself

Answer ②

20

A: Would you like to go window-shopping at the mall to-day?

B: You know we never just window-shop. One of us always picks something up that is (   ).

A: I know. At least we always hunt for bargains.

B: Like the time we bought up all those cheap woolen socks!

① sold-out

② in refund policy

③ for a full refund

④ on sale

Answer ④

※ 다음 우리말을 영어로 옮긴 것 중 옳지 않은 것은? [21~29]

21 ① 어떤 드레싱을 원하십니까?

= What kind of dressing would you like?

② 내가 계산하겠습니다.

= Let me share the bill.

③ 마취가 깨면 좀 아플 겁니다.

= You will be in some pain when the anesthesia wears off.

④ 신고할 것이 있나요?

= Do you have anything to declare?

Answer ②(나누어 냅시다.) → Let me pick up the tab.

22　① 꼬집어서 말씀 드릴 수 없습니다.

　　　= It doesn't make any sense at all.

　　② 나를 바람 맞추지 마라.

　　　= Don't stand me up.

　　③ 잘한다. 바로 그거야.

　　　= There you go.

　　④ 가끔 소식을 전해줘.

　　　= Drop me a line once in a while.

　　Answer　①(말이 전혀 안됩니다.) → I can't put my fingers on it.

23　① 너는 그럴 자격이 된다.

　　　= You derserve it.

　　② 꼴 좋다[인과응보].

　　　= Serves you right.

　　③ 속도 좀 줄여라.

　　　= Step on it.

　　④ 내일 쉬어도 되나요?

　　　= Can I take a day off tomorrow?

　　Answer　③(속도 좀 내라.) → Slow down.

24　① 날 바보로 만들지 마.

　　　= Don't make a fool of me.

② 네가 자초한 일이야.

= You asked for it.

③ 재촉하지 마라.

= He has a short fuse.

④ 왜 나한테 화풀이야?

= Why are you taking it out on me?

nswer ③(그는 성미가 급하다./그는 화를 잘 낸다.) → Don't rush me.

25 ① 그는 불끈 화를 냈어.

= He went into his tantrums.

② 더 이상은 못 참아.

= He's a real pain in the neck.

③ 당신 일이나 신경 쓰세요!

= Mind your own business!

④ 그 사람 진짜 날 신경 쓰이게 하네.

= He really gets on my nerves.

nswer ②(그는 골칫거리입니다.) → Enough is enough.

26 ① 있잖아?

= Guess what?

② 그걸 꼭 말로 해야 되니?

= Do I have to make it explicit?

③ 힘들어도 잘 견뎌!

   = What a coincidence!

④ 소름 끼친다.

   = That gives me gooseflesh[goose bumps].

Answer ③(정말 우연이군요!) → Hang in there!

27 ① 내가 커피를 끓여줄게.

   = I will fix you some coffee.

② 내가 힘 좀 썼지.

   = Please accept my condolences.

③ 진심이야.

   = I mean it.

④ 으스스하다.

   = It gives me the (cold) creeps.

Answer ②(삼가 조의를 표합니다.) → I pulled some strings.

28 ① 감 잡았어!

   = There is something fishy about it.

② 온 몸이 쑤신다.

   = My whole body aches all over.

③ 그래도 그만하길 다행이다.

   = It could have been worse than that.

④ 나도 정말 그러고 싶었는데, 그럴 수가 없었어.

= I was dying to do it, but I couldn't.

Answer ①(그거 수상한 냄새가 나는데.) → I got the idea. / I've got the hang of it.

29 ① 배가 부르니 가벼운 후식이 어때?

= Now that we are stuffed, what about some light desserts?

② 둘 다 모두 가질 수는 없다.

= You can't eat your cake and have it.

③ 제때의 바늘 한 번이 아홉 바느질을 던다.

= A stitch in time saves nine.

④ 김칫국부터 마시지 마라.

= Great oaks from little acorns grow.

Answer ④(천 리 길도 한걸음부터) → Don't count the chicken before they are hatched.

※ 다음 소방관련 용어 중 표현이 바르지 못한 것을 고르시오. [30~33]

30 ① 소방사: Firefighter

② 소방교: Senior firefighter

③ 소방장: Captain/Fire sergeant

④ 소방위: Second lieutenant/Assistant fire chief

Answer ④(소방령) → Senior captain/Fire lieutenant

31　① 안전벨트: Safety belt

　　② 들것: Ascender

　　③ 이동식 발전기: Portal generator

　　④ 연기투시기: Smoke flashlight

　　Answer　②(승강기) → Stretcher

32　① 체온계: Blood press gauge

　　② 골절부목: Fracture splint

　　③ 머리고정대: Head harness

　　④ 후두경: Laryngoscope

　　Answer　①(혈압계) → Thermometer

33　① 구조대: Rescue team

　　② 발화점: Flashing point

　　③ 감전: Electric shock

　　④ 소방검사: Fire inspection

　　Answer　②(인화점) → Ignition point

필수 영어 속담

IV

소방공무원을 위한
현장생활영어

1 첫 술에 배부르랴.

○ Rome was not built in a day.

2 시작이 반이다.

○ Well begun is half done.

3 소귀에 경 읽기

○ Talking to the wall.

4 돌다리도 두들겨 보고 건너라.

○ Look before you leap.

5 개천에서 용 난다.

○ From rags to riches./A rags-to-riches story.

6 손뼉도 부딪혀야 소리가 난다. = 혼자서는 할 수 없다.

○ It takes two to tango.

7 일석이조

○ Kill two birds with one stone.

8 울며 겨자 먹기

○ Biting the bullet.

털어서 먼지 안 나는 사람 없다.

- ○ Everyone has a skeleton in the[his] closet[cupboard].

일각이 여삼추

- ○ A minute is like three years.
- ○ Every minute seems like a thousand.

자업자득

- ○ Face the music.
- ○ He got what he bargained for.
- ○ As you make your bed, so you must lie upon it.

아니 땐 굴뚝에 연기 날까

- ○ No smoke without fire.

낮말은 새가 듣고 밤말은 쥐가 듣는다.

- ○ Walls have ears.

공자 앞에서 문자 쓴다.

- ○ To teach a fish how to swim.

쥐구멍에도 볕들 날 있다.

- ○ Every dog has his day.

16 헌 짚신도 짝이 있다.

○ Every Jack has his Jill.

17 제 눈에 안경이다.

○ Beauty is in the eye of the beholder.

18 빈손으로 왔다가 빈손으로 간다(空手來空手去).

○ Shrouds have no pockets.

○ Naked came we into the world and naked shall we depart from it.

19 구관이 명관이다.

○ Better the devil you know than the devil you don't know.

20 굴러온 돌이 박힌 돌 뺀다.

○ Bad money drives out good.

21 금상첨화(錦上添花)

○ Icing on the cake.

22 부전자전(父傳子傳)

○ Like father, like son.

○ The apple doesn't fall far from the tree.

상부상조(相扶相助)

- One hand washes the other.
- You scratch my back, I'll scratch yours.

소문만복래(笑門萬福來)

- If you laugh, blessings will come your way.

약육강식(弱肉強食)

- Big fish eat little fish.

조금이라도 빗나간 것은 빗나간 것이다(五十步百步).

- A miss is as good as a mile.

오월동주(吳越同舟)

- Adversity makes strange bedfellows.

이열치열(以熱治熱)

- Fight fire with fire.

자화자찬(自畵自讚)

- Blowing one's own horn[trumpet].

전화위복(轉禍爲福)

- Every cloud has a silver lining

  (먹구름도 뒤쪽은 은빛으로 빛난다.)

31 죽마고우(竹馬故友)

- A buddy from my old stomping grounds.

32 진퇴양난(進退兩難)

- Between a rock and a hard place.

33 천생연분(天生緣分)

- Match made in heaven.

34 촌철살인(寸鐵殺人)

- Brevity is the soul of wit.

35 침소봉대(針小棒大)

- Making a mountain out of a molehill.
- Making mountains out of molehills.

36 사공이 많으면 배가 산으로 올라간다.

- Too many cooks in the kitchen.
- Too many cooks spoil the broth.

37 견물생심(見物生心)

- Opportunity makes a thief.

38 고진감래(苦盡甘來)

- After a storm comes a calm.

사상누각(沙上樓閣)

- Castle in the air.

금강산도 식후경

- Empty sacks will never stand upright.
- A loaf of bread is better than the song of many birds.

연목구어(緣木求魚)

- You can't get blood from a stone.

돼지 목에 진주 목걸이

- Casting pearls before swine.

등잔 밑이 어둡다.

- The husband is always the last to know.

똥 묻은 개가 겨 묻은 개 나무란다.

- The pot calls the kettle black.

못 먹는 감 찔러나 본다.

- Sour grapes.

미인박명(美人薄命)

- Whom the gods love die young.

47 원숭이도 나무에서 떨어질 때가 있다.

    ❂ (Even) Homer sometimes nods.

48 종로에서 뺨 맞고 한강에 가서 눈 흘긴다.

    ❂ Go home and kick the dog.

49 제 버릇 개 못 준다.

    ❂ A leopard cannot change his spots.

50 세월은 사람을 기다리지 않는다.

    ❂ Time and tide wait(s) for no man.

저자약력

노이균

KBS 제1라디오 '노이균의 생활영어' 진행
고려대학교에서 영문학(영시) 전공
The University of Edinburgh에서 영문학(영시) 전공
The University of California, Los Angeles에서 TESL(Teaching
English as a Second Language) 전공

소방공무원을 위한 현장생활영어

2018년 8월 10일 초판 1쇄 인쇄
2018년 8월 15일 초판 1쇄 발행

지은이 노이균
펴낸이 진욱상
펴낸곳 (주)백산출판사
교 정 편집부
본문디자인 구효숙
표지디자인 오정은

저자와의
합의하에
인지첩부
생략

등 록 2017년 5월 29일 제406-2017-000058호
주 소 경기도 파주시 회동길 370(백산빌딩 3층)
전 화 02-914-1621(代)
팩 스 031-955-9911
이메일 edit@ibaeksan.kr
홈페이지 www.ibaeksan.kr

ISBN 979-11-88892-70-9   13740
값 15,000원